KU-191-422

Words on the Level

BY THE SAME AUTHOR

Autobiography
Old and Young

Word Books

A Word in Your Ear
Just Another Word
I Give You My Word
I Break My Word
A Word in Edgeways
Words in Season
Mind Your Language
A Ring of Words
A Rhapsody of Words
Chosen Words
Random Words
A Charm of Names

General

Shakespeare
How Shakespeare Spent the Day
Shakespeare in His Time
The Women in Shakespeare's Life
Shakespeare and the Actors
Shakespeare: a Profile
Dickens in His Time
Bernard Shaw in His Time
Dark Ladies
Balmoral
The Way of My World
Summer in Scotland
Winter in London
London
Looking at Theatres
Theatre 1954–5
Theatre 1955–6

and much else

WORDS ON THE LEVEL

IVOR BROWN

THE BODLEY HEAD

LONDON SYDNEY

TORONTO

© Ivor Brown 1973
ISBN 0 370 10241 X
Printed and bound in Great Britain for
The Bodley Head Ltd
9 Bow Street, London WC2E 7AL
by William Clowes & Sons Ltd, Beccles
Set in Linotype Baskerville
First published 1973

Foreword

The equalitarians are in charge. Sameness is all. Incomes must be assimilated. It is urged that all children must go to the same kind of school. After unischool comes unisex. Our young men and women like to be indistinguishable. Distinction has become a word in disgrace. The English language, which once could show its fat, must be 'put on a lean diet'. T. S. Eliot used those words of his own poetic method. To use rare or difficult words is thought to be a form of class distinction; it is snobbish and so chargeable with the sin of pride. The ownership and display of a large vocabulary is as much resented by the levellers as the possession of large property.

'Wealth', said Bacon, 'is like muck, not good unless it be spread.' That is wise and acceptable counsel. Now education, the manure of our young minds, must be equally dispersed. That too is agreed and we are all the time putting the comprehensive principle into wider practice. The methods of communication have been radically changed since broadcasting of the spoken word began fifty years ago. The change of verbal usage in the projection of news and views was still more drastic when television drew millions of viewers to get their facts as well as their fun from the fireside 'box'. Another result of this treasure in the home was the increased use of chairs and sofas. A nation of lookers-in is increasingly a nation of 'telly' sitters. They are on the same level as their screen. Nothing must be said, at least in the programmes of general appeal, which can be described as 'over people's heads'. The speakers are also squatters, sitting round a table when a subject is being discussed with all types of opinion equally represented.

The political orators and the academic lecturers in their several premises stand above us on a platform or a dais. Those who guide us on the screen through a foreign country and tell us of its home life or, more excitingly, of its wild life may be walk-and-talk men on their travels but they often deliver their report from a chair. Even if the subject is mountaineering only the climbers are seen in altitude. We take no more exercise than the shifting of a cushion on the couch. When bored we have the unquestioned privilege of turning a knob and so putting the man of authority, be he professor or politician, in his place. Equality could not go further.

With levelling of status comes levelling of posture. Even the tiny difference in height between a standing and a sedentary speaker is noticed. It may be resented by the sitters. Standing can be a handicap to the person who is talking because it makes him seem a superior person. That was frankly stated by Lord Clark in a lecture which he gave to the Royal Society of Literature. 'If to save myself trouble I insert into a television script a phrase or two from a lecture, I always have to remove it in performance. So much is this a psychological matter that I find it difficult to do a good television performance standing up—the posture alone makes me speak in a more pretentious style.' There is excessive modesty in that. From what I know of his excellent writing he has never been intellectually aloof or self-important. But his view that to be

6

erect instead of sedentary creates alienation from an audience is significant. To keep language on the level limbs must be on the level too. Nothing, not even a speaker's profile, must be an inch above our heads.

To me it seems that one who combines the encyclopaedic knowledge of the arts and of their place in the enrichment of human society in many ages and countries with the mastery of communication which Lord Clark showed in his widely and justly valued television series on Civilisation has the right to stand above our less instructed selves. In the cultural world, to use an adjective which he may dislike is hard to replace, he is one of those whom the Scots call 'high heid yins', but I should not mind if he towered over me physically as well as in sense and sensibility. But one has to bear in mind his belief that he who talks to millions is put at a disadvantage by even a trifling difference in height. I do not agree that to be up on a dais or a stage is to be 'uppity' in manner. But here was one who thinks that to be so, and he speaks from experience and with human sympathy in a world devoted to the principle of 'all alike'.

When Lord Clark made his remark about posture his lecture carried the title of 'Mandarin English'. Mandarin was a term frequently used by Arnold Bennett in his literary criticism. He applied it in a disparaging way to the Big Bow-Wows, as Sir Walter Scott called them, of the literary and particularly the academic world. He hated the approach to books of the pundit who was more concerned to exhibit his erudition than to inform and assist the general reader. Lord Clark's definition of Mandarin English keeps clear of this sweeping dislike. For him 'it is the diction of a ruling minority, formed by the study of dead languages and used in the conduct of foreign affairs . . .'. It 'goes back to

7

the middle of the eighteenth century and begins with Gibbon'. For nearly two centuries it powerfully prevailed among those known as 'Men of Letters'. They assumed a degree of taste and knowledge which was the same as their own. They addressed even this elevated public from above, writing, as it were, with their desks set on a dais.

A democratic society is rightly intolerant of this 'apartheid' of the high priests of culture from the laity who want to be told about the events and practice of politics as well as about books worth reading, music worth hearing and plays and films worth seeing. To meet that desire, which is not universal although it is felt by an increasing minority of the public, the language of the writers, and specially of the broadcasting speakers, must be adjusted to the limited power of general comprehension.

The old mandarins have gone and so have the new. Their successors have made learning more accessible, as it should be. But there is loss of quality in the language, if any kind of verbal amplitude and decoration is vetoed in the process of popularising the subjects once restricted to the enclaves of scholarship where town and gown were not on meeting terms. To me, as a student of words, fascinated by their sound in the ear as much as by their appearance on paper, this is a serious deprivation. I admit the social value of linguistic levelling. I regret the starvation of 'the lean diet'.

I also owe to the Mandarin lecture already quoted a reminder of a striking statement by Sir Henry Wootton in his *Elements of Architecture*: 'Well-building hath three conditions, commodity, firmness, delight.' By commodity he meant convenience and approachability. The Mandarin English was not always that. The Bow-Wows were not inviting all to their kennel. There was majesty, but as with a range of lofty and admired mountains, altitude keeps it aloof. At least for some readers the structure brings the pleasure of a pattern. The mandarins were composers as well as builders. Their deliberately contrived sentences, especially those of Edward Gibbon, were pieces of music. Sonority has its own delight, providing what musicians call a diapason, which is defined as 'compass of voice or instrument, music written in harmony, a rich swelling sound'. The necessary vocabulary could not be rationed like the items of diet for those banting.

There was once an esteemed possession vaguely called Style. Dean Swift in his *Letter to a Young Clergyman* shrewdly defined this as 'proper words in proper places'. For the mandarins it was not so disciplined. It was something large and lofty which the young men were expected to acquire. I remember two remarks made by the Master of Balliol, J. L. Strachan-Davidson, who shared in the task of the other dons to whom freshmen had to take a weekly essay on a political or literary topic. When Trevenen Huxley, the sadly short-lived brother of Sir Julian and Aldous, read him a piece of wordy undergraduate cleverness, 'Strachan', who obviously did not like the matter but was struck by the method, said in his curious purring voice, 'Mr Huxley, you have a spark of style.' To me he said only that I lacked style and could acquire it by reading Ruskin, then considered by the addicts of Mandarin English to be the supreme stylistic model.

Such advice is never, I think, given now. Style is worse than suspect. It is a dead dog, like Bow-Wow prose and poetry. Swift's edict abides for sensible writers of today, but the proper words are now austerely limited to the language of daily use, flat stuff for a flattened society, broadcasters' lingo, spoken on the level, for the squatters by a squatter. There is a hint of height about Style with a capital S, and that will never do.

When the ample and august English of the mandarins had gone out of fashion and the head-in-air authors were being succeeded by the down-to-earth writers and speakers, there was a short period in which the aesthetes cultivated a deliberately elaborate and decorated style. In this the choice of language was elegant and sometimes exotic. If 'Art for Art's Sake' was an acceptable idea, why not 'Words for Words' Sake'? The verbal profusion was not limited to the precious few. Oscar Wilde, capricious in his vocabulary as well as in his way of life, was soon read by many. To be as foppish in diction as in dress became a Chelsea fashion.

The young Max Beerbohm, whose volume of essays amusingly entitled *Works* appeared in 1896 when he was only twenty-four, paid in this book a salute to famous dandies and did so in an appropriately dandiacal prose. Later in life he could show his adaptability to the new and austere regimen of the microphones. On several occasions he delivered broadcasts which could not possibly be called 'uppity'. He levelled his language to suit the size of his audience. When he began his career in the higher journalism immediately after leaving Oxford he relished and sometimes perfected the manner of the *Yellow Book* period. He indulged in the flourish of a fine phrase. There was affectation in his display of latinity. For him jockeys on a racecourse were 'homuncules scudding oe'r the vert', and when he wrote *Zuleika Dobson* a quarter of a century later he called Oxford undergraduettes 'virgincules'. In his praise of the titivation of feminine faces he called the colour of rouge the 'vermeil tint' which would 'ensorcel the eyes of the beholder'. His sad folk were tristful and for sweetness he wrote dulcitude or dulcedo. He used secernment for separation and accessancy for increase. It seems silly now, but when I re-read 'Max'

I find his preciosity more entertaining than exasperating. There have been these trends of alternation between the exalted and the level.

In the Elizabethan period there had been a delight in verbal exhibitionism and foppishness in the choice of phrase. It was exemplified and ridiculed by Shakespeare in *Love's Labour's Lost*. The pedantic Don Armado, who dotes on strange words, is described as 'too picked, too spruce and too peregrinate' in his conversation. Peregrinate, which is defined as 'foreign-fashioned or having the air of a traveller', was approved by the curate, Sir Nathaniel, as 'a most singular and choice epithet'. The Shakespearian verdict is against the picked and spruce speech. Berowne forswears 'taffeta phrases, silken terms precise' and decides that his wooing must henceforward be expressed in 'russet yeas and honest kersey noes'. Shakespeare, while discarding the pretentious phrase-making which he had mocked, remained a supreme innovator in adding to the language and in doing so utilised the flow of words coming to England from Europe, especially from Italy, as a result of the Renaissance.

Inflation has become a word of menace because it robs money of its meaning. Recent changes have also deprived our vocabulary by reducing the names of our coinage to the dreary pounds, which buy little, and the pence which buy nothing. A few years ago we had the old and agreeable variety of crowns, half-crowns, florins and shillings which followed the golden splendour of the medieval angels and nobles. While we are fighting monetary inflation, we should stop the deflation of the dictionary.

It may be replied that length at least is being restored to some of the lingo often met in the newspapers and in the jargon of the public relations officers and the tycoons of the advertising industry

11

who tell us what to believe, where to go and what to buy. They have, like the journalists, taken a fancy to polysyllabic nouns and adjectives. Has there been a subconscious feeling that the mean little brevities of levelled English are creating a sense of word-starvation? Whatever the reason there has been an influx of the lengthy, presumably because it is thought to add importance to the news-story or the salesman's message. Why otherwise should 'escalate' have replaced the simple 'rise'? When it first appeared I thought it was too pompous to last. But escalation continues to escalate. Another recent favourite has been encapsulate. Nothing can be simply inserted. I read that 'an important clause has been encapsulated in a Bill now being discussed in Parliament'. We have become a nation of pill-swallowers and tablet devotees, whether the need is to sleep or to keep awake. So the capsule is a familiar article in the home. But the verb is being absurdly overworked.

Another nuisance is polarity. People and things are not kept apart or separated. They have to be polarised, as though we were living in the Arctic circle. Equally tiresome is the trendy orientation. It should mean facing east, but all sense of geography has gone. An 'advanced' thinker is leftward-orientated.

This form of amplifying our shrivelled language is far from being a gain. I want enrichment not enlargement. The mandarins and aesthetes have been discredited as too formal and even formidable in one case and too foppish and fantastic in the other. If the level is to be raised, not escalated, the diction of our poets since the Middle Ages provides a storehouse of words which have colour and melody. It should be raided for its fine-looking and fine-sounding contents. The verbal flowers of the anthologies are not faded beyond rescue.

Ambragious and Waffle

Ambragious talk, not likely to be so described now, is tricky. There was a noun ambrage which meant more than profuse and incompetent ambiguity; it was deliberate and deceptive. I have read of a copious speaker being called ambragious, which was inaccurate unless he was leading his listeners astray as well as far afield.

The levellers have cut down to size the old and polysyllabic terms for tedious word-spinning. From the Greek came macrology to describe length without depth in speech-making. Classical too are periphrastic, prolix and pleonastic.

For adding vagueness to verbosity we have adopted a name from the larder, waffle. As an addition to the tea-table it is 'a crisp kind of batter-cake cooked in an iron-mould with honey or syrup added'. Some learned elders could call it sapid; the young might prefer to say scrumptious, an admirable invention to describe a rich confection. The transference of waffle to a long and cloudy speech has been well justified. It suggests the sticky verbiage in which the talker or writer conceals the absence of clear thinking. The wafflers are not ambragious by design. They go muddling on in a syrupy fashion, hoping to please all parties and offend none, but eventually boring all.

For variants we have the Scottish blethers, sometimes blathers, for rambling and foolish chatter. A waffler of this kind may be contemptuously called

13

a blatherskite. Also he may be said to haver. Havers in the plural is also a family name, once singularly inapposite in the case of a prominent barrister, no ambragious waffler, who became Havers, Q.C. I have not heard of a Mr Waffle. If there is one he can hardly dare to appear as an after-dinner speaker or on a political platform.

Androgynous

'How androgynous can we get?' said one who was looking at the young people in the street. To judge by his vocabulary he had obviously received a gentleman's education with special attention to Greek. The levelling process has reduced the size of the adjective applied to a crowd in which male and female are indistinguishable owing to the flowing locks reaching down to the shoulders and the similarity of the shabbily trousered legs. But the classics are not forgotten in our new terminology. We turn from Athens to Rome for our serviceable and easily understood Unisex.

Androgynous means 'uniting the qualities of both sexes'. So it could be a complimentary adjective for one who is both tough and tender, sympathetic to all the moods of humanity. It does not imply a physical combination of sexual features and organs. We have hermaphrodite for that. Homosexual is a misleading term in its most common usage. The homo part of it suggests likeness, but the members of a homosexual friendship or partnership are either a male of muscular appearance and another of feminine aspect and tendency, or a mannish-looking woman with a very feminine member of her sex. To the mannish woman the slang word 'butch' has recently been given. It is a nasty noun. We do better to keep our vocabulary classical. Hermaphrodite lifts us to their Olympus where Hermes and Aphrodite were certainly not homosexuals or androgynous.

Most of those who have justified the label Unisex are by no means homosexual. They practise normal sexual relations with such frequency and fertility that free advice and equipment for contraception are laid on by public authorities without the angry protests which would have been heard before the menace of over-population was realised.

Ancillary and Others

One does not expect trade unionists on strike to have a long Latin label which came from Roman domesticity and survives in an unlevelled and scholarly form. When the hospital assistants of many grades and functions were defying the financial freeze of 1973 they were constantly described as ancillary workers. They might have been called auxiliaries, but that term has had such a long association with armed forces that, if so called, they might have been taking up rifles instead of laying down mops. Auxiliaries are 'foreign and allied troops in the service of a nation at war'. Ancillaries have become 'civilian subordinates'. The ancient *ancilla* was a female servant in a Roman home or villa and doubtless was expected to be a maiden meek and mild. Oxford's first alternative for the adjective ancillary is subservient. This is strange since that is elsewhere defined as 'willing to adapt oneself to the wishes of others, obsequious, fawning'. The hospital ancillaries on strike, with pickets and protests round the gates, were certainly not crouching on bended knees in demure abasement.

Obsequious people did not begin as imitators of Uriah Heep. They were dutiful followers of accepted procedure. The funeral obsequies were salutes to the dead made in dignified propriety. No cringing was implied. The adjective was given a downward push and was increasingly applied to those who paraded their respect for their superiors in wealth and power.

Burial has attracted a considerable pomp in its vocabulary. The royal or illustrious corpse lay and still lies in state on a catafalque. That is described as 'medieval French of unknown derivation'. Lesser people have a monosyllable for their coffins. They lie, with little or no state, on a bier. In the case of the eminent the progress to the cemetery was accompanied by a cortège. The commoners were again deprived of a French word. Cortège was constantly met at one time in Press descriptions of an august funeral. I remember that when I was working for the *Manchester Guardian* many years ago, cortège and obsequies were banned in its book of verbal rules. I was told that the great editor C. P. Scott would not have pomposity in the reporting of funerals. Corpses were to be corpses not mortal remains, and coffins coffins and burials burials, not interments. Certainly there could be no mention of a cortège.

This levelling has now, I think, been widely followed. For the majestic lingo applicable by non-levelling authors there is a splendid example in Sir Thomas Browne's *Urn-Burial*, where the words are marshalled in a cortège.

Linguistic amplitude has been retained, whether the hospital workers like it or not, in the adjective ancillary. Since we have deviated into graveyards it may be suggested that the gravedigger in *Hamlet*

16

was ancillary to the maimed obsequies which the churlish priest said could not be 'enlarged' in Ophelia's case since her death was doubtful.

Apartheid and Aloof

The racialists, sometimes called racists, and their indignant opponents have imported the word Apartheid from South Africa. I shall have more to say of this in my note on Discrimination. For the vocabulary of apartness, isolation, and loneliness I prefer the poignant aloof. It has a nautical origin. In the years of sail to keep aloof was to hold the ship's head to the wind, whence came the verb to luff. The aloof mariner was 'away to windward'. The landlubbers took over the adjective long ago to describe those who liked to keep asunder. The verb remains at sea. Those who secede or resign from a cause or a faith do not luff. They are often said to opt out, a classicism strangely favoured by the levellers, who are not as a rule Latinists. If brevity there must be, why not leave or quit? In Communist countries those who opt for their own opinions are accused of deviation and usually doomed.

The sound of aloof has appealed to the poets. To Milton the moon was 'the great luminarie aloof from constellations thick'. Tennyson chose it as a synonym for distant. He saw 'purple cliffs aloof'. Ben Jonson used it with pride in his apartheid from the rival dramatists who were being preferred by the fickle Jacobean public at the end of his career as a playwright. In his 'Ode to Himself' he stated his professional policy for the coming years. He would leave the territory from which the nymphs of poetry had gone, now 'the seats and bowers by chattering pies defaced'. Ben thus stated his decision to become one of the theatre's opters-out,

> But since our dainty age
>   Cannot endure reproof
> Make not thyself a page
> To that strumpet, the Stage.
>   But sing high and aloof,
>   Safe from the wolf's black jaw and the dull
>   ass's hoof.

Behind lofty aloofness there is usually some melancholy. Here misanthropy is breaking in. Perhaps a night in jovial tavern company at the Mermaid relieved his disgust with the mingled menagerie of human magpies, wolves and donkeys of the Bankside world.

I remember hearing an amusing confusion of aloof with another curious word beginning with 'a'. A speaker describing a man who took a detached and superior line in company said, 'He always seems a bit akimbo.' That inexplicable term, meaning with one's hands on one's hips, has nothing to do with a head-in-air stance, but in this case it was understood to signify 'high and aloof'.

There was a time when wine-merchants wrote, or employed advertising copy-writers to compose, elegant tributes to their vintages, commending for example a 'consequential and truly episcopal port'. From James Agate came a neat parody of this nonsense, 'This claret is so distinguished as to be almost aloof.'

Apheliotropic

My botany is somewhat sketchy, but it has introduced me to a fine verbal mouthful which is applicable to the human fauna as well as to the floral bends and inclinations. Apheliotropic flowers are those which turn away from the sun. So do some people, who may be called heliophobes since they prefer the sombre shade to the solar blaze from which they shrink. In Britain they are now much fewer than they were. Earlier in this century those who could afford to travel made their escape from our climate in February or March and went to the South of France. There they moderately sunned themselves. To make the journey in summer was then unthinkable. Nor would they have dreamed of braving the heat on the Costa Brava of Spain's Mediterranean shores to which the horde of heliophils now resort for the pleasures (and some pains) of self-bakery.

The distrust of solar radiation among Victorians and Edwardians was brought home to me in my home. When I was looking for a house in Hampstead many years ago (and found one whose lease I bought) I was assured by an old lady then living there that one of the sitting-rooms was delightful because 'it never got any sun at all'. The upholstery was her chief concern. The sun faded fabrics. So the sun was a pest. She was keenly, one could hardly say ardently, apheliotropic. If she had to go into the possibly sunny street I am sure that she raised a protective parasol, a defensive implement now rarely carried. That word goes back to 1660. Were the mistresses of King Charles II sun-avoiders? The masculine sun-dodgers sheltered their heads in Panama hats. That name which arrived in the nineteenth century is described in the *O.E.D.* as 'a misnomer for a hat made from the undeveloped leaves of the seam-less screw-pines', a Central American tree.

A history of British distaste for exposure and the subsequent cult of it by nudists and sun-bathers could be interesting. For the heliophils another large classical word has been invented. They are Ecdysiasts. I owe that to the brilliant American journalism of H. L. Mencken. But he was writing about another kind of stripper, the ladies who provided a peculiar form of masculine excitement. They 'teased' to please, in their strip 'joints'. That word brings us down from the heights to levellers' English.

Arcane

Since I have been lamenting the limitation and flattening of the language I should be ready to praise and encourage any opposite tendency when I find it in my daily papers. The reporters of Parliamentary business I am happy to find on my side. They have recently taken to unusual adjectives and in this practice they follow one another. For example in three different journals I have within a few days seen allusion to the arcane details of the constitutional complications at Westminster. Secrecy is implied. The *Penguin Dictionary* omits the adjective but includes the noun *arcanum* and its plural *arcana*, 'a mystery, a hidden thing, a secret remedy or elixir'. Elixir is explained as 'an invigorating drink or strong cordial'. If we press this significance of the word arcane procedure might be more spirited than hugger-mugger, which was Shakespeare's adjective for the kind of concealment which we now call 'sweeping under the carpet'.

Another classical favourite of the political journalists is abrasive, which is defined as 'scratching or grinding'. If I have a rough shave with an old blade I am abraded. When the Opposition speakers are knifing or mauling the Government their speeches are said to be abrasive. Some of their remarks might be called catty. But dignity is given to the claws by abrasion. There is a contrast to this when a Minister is turning away wrath by giving a smooth answer and showing what a nice fellow he really is. Then he is reported to be showing his charisma. There is a puzzle about this word, which is now being wrongly applied to personal charm of the persuasive, ingratiating kind. In the opinion of Oxford it has nothing to do with mundane likeability. It was 'a favour specially vouchsafed by God' and later 'a grace or talent'. Penguin also looks to heaven and Parnassus for its meaning and describes it as 'theological, a spiritual gift, an exceptionally high degree of artistic genius'. This is very different from the capacity to smile one's way out of trouble, to appease opponents with suavity of manner, and to be 'a good mixer' at a party. 'Exceptional artistic genius'? It seems that one has to be a saint or a Shakespeare to qualify as charismatic. But I salute the eagerness displayed by the journalists in the Lobby and Gallery in no arcane fashion to lift their vocabulary above the general level.

Arcanity, if there is such a noun, is not a deliberate concealment. Clandestine conduct is a contrived secrecy. Here is a fine epithet of Latin origin which might be more often introduced. But few dramatists of today would use it in the title of a play as George Colman and David Garrick did in *The Clandestine Marriage* for which they collaborated in 1766. It contains a rich character part in Lord Ogleby of which Sir Donald Wolfit made the most. In its dialogue is some fine talk, such as the description of an elaborate piece of landscape gardening laced with sinuous ponds as 'all crinkum-crankum'. If I re-read the piece now I should not be surprised to find the matrimonial circumstances in the plot called arcane.

Balderdash, Bosh and Bunkum

Balderdash—'a senseless jumble of words'. But it had first been a repulsive jumble of liquids. Mixing one's drinks is usually unwise and the Elizabethans who spoke of a cup of balderdash and may even have ordered and absorbed it were taking in a gulp of 'milk and beer, beer and wine, etc.'. The 'etc.' suggests even further nastiness. It is not surprising that the name was transferred from the poorest of tipple to the poorest of talk, with which meaning it survives. Jumble, by the way, now a noun and often an adjective, especially when attached to the word sale, began as a verb meaning 'to move about in mingled disorder, to flounder'. One can imagine a drinker of balderdash jumbling to what he then called the jakes in order to get rid of the stuff. If milk was always an ingredient along with the ale and wine intoxication was less likely than nausea.

In our permissive vocabulary balderdash has become comparatively rare whereas a dismissive cry of balls is certain to be heard in any kind of society when remarks are being dismissed as rubbish. To judge by the plays, books, films and journalism of the nineteen-seventies with their endless discussion of sex with no words or facts barred, J. B. Priestley was accurately diagnosing the mental condition of our time when he said that we have gone sex-mad. It is therefore odd that, amid all the glorification of what is now called 'having sex', balls should be a contemptuous term for balderdash and bosh.

Ought not the word to be a complimentary welcome to manly, forthright and clear opinions?

An initial 'b' is a regular feature in contumelious words. Hence bastards, bitches and buggers are continually in our ears amid the expletives common in the conversation of all classes. Probably 'b' helped balderdash into its old favour. It has certainly assisted one of its successors, the blameless bosh.

That has had a varied usage with some rare meanings. It is 'part of a blast-furnace'. It is 'an outline or rough sketch'. As a verb it has meant to flaunt or cut a dash. But to us now it is silly stuff, trash, foolish talk. It sounds simple and native but the learned have traced an origin in the Near East by way of the Turkish word *Ayasha*. That seems to me to be far-fetched in both senses of the adjective. Whatever its birth, it did not arrive in Britain until the nineteenth century, at which time piffle was also being introduced as a description of verbal rubbish. That is an effective word. The 'p' helps. It is true that 'p' introduces many names of excellent things such as peace, perfect peace. But it fits well into the lingo of the despicable. Piffle, suggesting also a nasty smell, fits into the company of things paltry, putrid, poisonous, pestilent and piddling. I notice that another 'p' word has recently come into slang usage. That is 'plonk' for any cheap, rough wine.

We are back among the liquors where balderdash landed us. The vocabulary of abusive rejection of fatuous remarks has included several foods widely held in derision, although they may seem to some to be tasty enough. Thousands, though not in the 'U' class, relish a dish of tripe, which is one of the alternatives to bosh. Bologna's sausage has doubtless plenty of flavour but it has given us the slang boloney for drivel. Was poppy-cock, an American importation, once something edible but

23

not enjoyable? Eric Partridge suggests in a tentative way that the 'flamboyancy' of the poppy in the fields may have been the cause of its adoption. I doubt that. I return to my view of the baleful influence of the initial 'p'. Cock is one of the names for nonsense and poppy strengthens its dismissal.

Drivel began its downward motion as a form of dribble, a drip of saliva, and moved on from the oral flux to the verbal folly. Drip in today's slang is both nonsense and the person who speaks it, the weak and stupid fellow who is also known as 'a wet'. I come back to the 'b's', with which balderdash started me on these ruminations among the rubbish. There is bilge and there is bunk, short for bunkum, a form of Buncombe. Buncombe is a district in North Carolina whose political representative decided that he must make a speech 'because Buncombe expected it'. That unfortunate place has been remembered in two continents for its member's dutiful resolve to do his stint of spouting even though the product was bosh or rubbish, which is a derivative of rubble, the fragments of a decaying or destroyed building.

Bougainvillaea and Others

Our list of flower-names contains some titles of imposing length, providing us with a mouthful as well as an eyeful. If the name of the gardener who introduced a new species is formidable there is no shrinking from it in dismay. The pioneer is honoured by the retention of all his syllables with two further letters added, usually 'ia' or 'ea'. Levelling does not intrude, at least in the higher grade of horticulture. A notable example is eschscholtzia, 'a Californian genus of herbaceous plants with bright yellow flowers'. It was first grown in Germany in 1857 by J. F. von Eschscholtz. When there was a vogue for Spelling Bee competitions on sound radio, in one or two of which I took part, we were sure to be confronted with that. Expecting it, I did my homework, and once forgot it.

Bougainvillaea, named after a French navigator called Bougainville who died in 1811, is described as 'a genus of tropical plants having flowers almost concealed by large, leafy bracts'. Sub-tropical would surely be a more accurate adjective, since in novels and short stories with a French Riviera background there is always a blaze of bougainvillaea. Ample visibility is assumed and the idea of a nearly total concealment by the tiresome bulky bracts must be questioned. The authors were presumably drawing on fact when they painted the scenes of their fiction with plentiful colour in a playground of characters and conduct far from colourless. While reading a short story by Angus Wilson about a prosperous family reunion in a country-house in Natal, I read of the rich floral surroundings with 'splashes of purple and crimson' provided by the bougainvillaea. There was no concealment there. He also mentioned the richly decorative poinsettia which we owe to J. R. Poinsett, an American diplomat who served in Mexico in the middle of the last century. It has 'scarlet floral leaves and yellow flowers'. There are many other and some lengthy examples of personally based flower-names which have not been shortened to suit the timidity of those who dislike any verbal prolixity.

Bougainvillaea has remained chiefly an alien to English gardens but, since Cornwall was at one time much advertised as the English Riviera, it may be discovered there in some sheltered niche despite the fact that the county's (or duchy's)

25

climate can as often be as 'misty-moisty' as it may be radiant for the midsummer strippers.

If bougainvillaea became better known in Britain our levellers might get to work on it. 'What a smashing boogie,' they might say. But that, with or without woogie added, is a dance not a decoration.

Boy and Girl

It is strange how little we know about some of the words which we hear and use most often in everyday conversation. I like to know how and why they got there. Not many people share my curiosity about verbal origins, but wondering about them and looking for information has become my hobby. Fortunately it is harmless, cheap, and sufficiently interesting to the few with a similar taste to make it worth while continuing to combine my personal fancy with my senile addiction to scribbling on.

Here are two nouns in constant use, boy and girl. Most take them for granted. But in my crotchety way I start wondering about their source and find there is a puzzle here. Even the word-wise Oxford scholars are baffled. 'Origin obscure' is the verdict in both cases. There is a tentative suggestion that boy came from Friesland. Whence the girl arrived evokes not even that amount of slender surmise.

To Anglo-Indians and other white Orientals the boy was a native servant, his age being immaterial. To the late Victorian reveller the boy was champagne, which puts him at the top of the wine-list. (Mention of vintage valuations reminds me of a supposedly academic gathering in the city of Durham to which the county's schoolmasters, assembled nominally for culture and more congenially for bodily refreshment, invited me to give a platform talk and take a tavern seat afterwards. There was much contentious argument about the rival merits and potency of the Northern and Southern brews of beer, on which topic I remained tactfully silent. Then one of the company suddenly said to me, 'Mr Brown, what do you mak of wine?' When I remarked that there were many kinds of wine and that I could not express an opinion which covered them all, he said simply, 'I mak it sissy stooff.' So much for the learned articles and vintage valuations of the 'Bon Viveur' journalists. The grape was out. So was the bubbly. The hop was in, and to hell with those sissies, the oenophiles.)

No 'bottle of the boy' for my Durham pedagogue. Even at a wedding feast he would have his pint or quart of beer (Northern) which to him was the proper potion of a man. If he had been a Johnsonian scholar, which I doubt, he could have added to the Doctor's classifications of claret as a liquor for boys, port for men and brandy for heroes. Champagne had not arrived then. If it had been familiar as the necessary companion of social celebration, it would not have appealed to the Grand Cham, whose assessment of the liquids and their potencies was the odd verdict of a tea-drinker. 'The boy' indeed! 'Mouthwash for the girls' he might have called it.

The boy has had a rather sad history in slang. Eric Partridge has discovered that it was a hump on the back, and that one so afflicted could be spoken of as 'he and his boy'. That is dated at 1800 and described as 'lower class'. I should be surprised to meet it now. Boy was used as a verb by Shakespeare who had the players of his feminine parts in mind. Cleopatra has her grim foreboding about the public degradation of her grand passion and the great days and nights with Antony:

> The quick comedians
> Extemporally will stage us and present
> Our Alexandrian revels. Antony
> Shall be brought drunken forth and I shall see
> Some squeaking Cleopatra boy—my greatness
> I' the posture of a whore.

That was an awkward speech for the boy playing the part. Might it not get a laugh and even a shout of 'Squeaker' from some ill-mannered member of the audience, of whose churlish 'gags' and interventions there is plenty of contemporary evidence? To be 'one of the boys' with a seat at the side of the stage was to practise what is now called 'audience participation' and approved by the opponents of the curtained theatre in which the separated public was prepared to listen politely.

Girl has also been a verb but not a pleasant one. Lechers have gone girling. As a noun, too, girl has been constantly used in slang with an unpleasant meaning. I remember the protest of a misunderstood party in the musical show *Guys and Dolls*,

> Take back your mink,
> Take back your pearls,
> What made you think
> That I was one of those girls?

There is further mystery with those who are called brisky juvenals in *A Midsummer Night's Dream*. The word lad is marked 'origin obscure' by Oxford. There is some light upon his partner, lass, which has been traced to Scandinavia. Lady had an old English start and not a lordly one. The word was linked with loaf, the kitchen or the bakery. No milady at first, she was the one who kneaded the dough.

Chagrin

'Hear me and touch Belinda with chagrin.' Alexander Pope's request would have been hard on the lady's cheek, assuming that to be the place of contact, if the origin for this term for mortification and discomfiture were known and remembered. Chagrin was first a form of shagreen, 'a species of untanned leather with a rough granular surface'. It could be taken from the hide of a horse or donkey but was chiefly the defensive coating of a shark, scratchy stuff, though now esteemed for ladies' handbags. Those who have been in some way scraped or wounded rarely choose this picturesque word for their distress. Afflicted persons, when put out of public life, are rarely so literate as to use it. I have never heard a politician who has been ejected from a position of power and profit explain to the interviewer that he was suffering chagrin.

That is partly because he has to conceal his humiliation with some routine bluff, partly because the language of Westminster is limited to the drab range of levelled English. Yet he might possibly say that he had undergone 'a traumatic experience', because the psychoanalysts have made the Greek word for a wound familiar. This classic darling of the soul-soother's couch has been widely adopted, like euphoria and euphoric for the pleasant and directly opposite sensation, by a large number of people who are lifting from the 'psycho' specialists many fragments of their jargon without knowing their source. The fewer the recipients of a classical education the more its vocabulary is being employed. A physical or emotional condition is now sometimes called a diathesis. I prefer the chagrin of a big-wig who has been demoted to the traumatic diathesis of a potentate who has become redundant. The humbler unemployed have now to be thus described to save them from the chagrin of the sack. Does this really comfort them or induce euphoria?

An ancient Greek word for the alleviation of a trauma is anodyne. It sounds well and fits well, without pedantry, into a line of English verse. In Matthew Arnold's *The Scholar Gypsy* one 'who most has suffered'

> Tells us his misery's birth and growth and signs,
> And how the dying spark of hope was fed,
> And how the breast was soothed, and how the head,
> And all his hourly varied anodynes.

That word puts a pill into poetry. In these lines one sees and hears the sad muttering of an ejected tenant of No 10 Downing Street. But his consolation is substantial. He can sell his Memoirs for a colossal price to soothe his chagrin.

Chapel

There is much that is peculiar about the various uses of this word. It has come to us from the Latin *capella*, a cloak, and there is a special connection with the cloak of Saint Martin which was kept in a sanctuary and guarded by the *Capellanus* who has given his name to our chapels and chaplains. The fourth-century saint had been a soldier in the reign of Constantine the Great. On obtaining his discharge he became a disciple of Saint Hilary, Bishop of Poitiers. He then founded a monastery, became Bishop of Tours, and the patron saint of travellers. The flourishing tourist industry might well have its head office in St Martin's Lane.

So the chapel has its 'holy Roman' origin. Yet in Britain none have been more tenaciously anti-Roman than the Protestant Nonconformists known as 'Chapel folk' who rebelled, first at great personal risk, against the domination of the Church of England. Their simple places of worship proudly kept to the name of chapel to distinguish them from the churches. Their pastors and ministers were obviously unaware of the word's (to them polluted) source. Yet, confusion again, the Anglicans kept the word for sanctuaries in their abbeys and cathedrals. The Lady Chapel in Westminster Abbey is one of its architectural glories. The Vatican itself has its world-famous Sistine Chapel.

I was led to investigate the various employments of this noun by the mystery of its application to groups of trade unionists engaged in the production of newspapers. The various grades of printers are organised in chapels with a Father of the Chapel at the head of each. The National Union of Journalists also has its chapels and paternal chairmen in all newspaper offices. I doubt whether any member of these bodies could explain how the word was adopted for the Trade Union branches whose members are concerned, often contentiously, with the hours, conditions, and rewards of their work. That it is an antique is shown by the fact that in 1688 'journeymen printers' were said 'to hold a chapel'. Were they all dissenters from the Anglican

31

faith, transferring to secular matters the vocabulary of their sectarian creed and its name for their places of worship?

Clichés which Cling

Old clichés never die nor do they fade away. I still hear it said that 'a clever lawyer could drive a coach and horses' through the wording of some measure which is on its way to becoming an Act of Parliament. Why are the sagacious attorneys taken to be so curiously faithful to that kind of transport? If they look out of their windows overlooking Lincoln's Inn Fields they have a delightful view of an old pleasaunce with a soothing, rustic name. But they are unlikely to see a horse and certain not to see a coach, a vehicle now only occasionally put on the road for a special occasion by a lonely and wealthy conservationist, probably on the way to Richmond, or by the grooms at the Palace for the spectacular service of Royalty on its way to Westminster for a coronation, a wedding or the opening of a new Parliamentary session.

Motor-coaches, especially in the tourist season, clog the town, but the cliché-mongers seem never to be aware of them. They remain in the world of the four-in-hand and the gentlemen who handled 'the ribbons'. So legislation is never threatened with the invasine dine of a motor-lorry. The garage is forgotten and the stable remembered, when the clichés are being trotted out, a suitable description in this case.

Fidelity to the nag and its harness continues in the names of the public-houses. The brewers are as obstinately horse-conscious as the politicians. My suburban High Street is jammed with motor-cars and foul with their fumes, but if I want to escape into a tavern for refreshment, the name over the door is 'The Nag's Head' or 'The Coach and Horses'. Does anybody call for a drink at a house called 'The Sparking Plug' or 'The Accelerator'? The place may have been garishly modernised and illuminated with some odious new 'fairy lights'. But the title on the door does not admit the arrival of petrol and electricity. There used to be back rooms where the old customers assembled for a pint and a gab. There was a murmur of local gossip, no shouting. This sombre parlour was called the Snug. The word has a cosy sound. It must be kept short. Snuggery is repulsive. How did it get there? The etymologists, probably no snug-addicted malt-worms, do not know. We are back with 'origin obscure'.

Those with conservative tastes may decide that this equestrian loyalty is an excellent thing and bless the stick-in-the-traces vocabulary. In clinging to herbage the cliché lingers in the vanishing countryside. For example, we are always hearing of grass roots. During some recent political Party Conferences, of which television made me a some-what transient auditor and spectator, the commen-tators were continually talking of the ordinary trade unionist as a grass-roots Labour supporter, almost certainly a townsman. There was talk of grass-roots Toryism too, a phrase perhaps more justified. What was absurd was the announcement that the problems of slum-clearance and re-housing must be tackled at the grass roots. I got the idea that the speaker, who probably came from one of our industrial Coketown conurbations, was a prac-tising farmer.

But there is one cliché which has moved with the times and into the mechanical workshop. Nobody throws a spade into the works. It is always a spanner.

Committee and Committed

Here is a word of weariness for many who have allowed themselves to be put on committees and then have dutifully served and sometimes perceptibly slept on them. There was a time when it was fashionable to speak of a Working Party; that was fair enough; the labour of keeping awake through a long afternoon when the chairman was inadequately coping with and failing to quench some loquacious and obstructive members justified the title. At one time, I have discovered, a Committee could be a single individual. In 1765 that was the legal name for 'a person to whom the charge of a lunatic or idiot is committed'. A sinister start.

The adjective committed has had some vicissitudes. It has long been applied to prisoners in gaol. It has recently been used of people holding strong opinions. The writer of a book or play is called committed when he is known to be doctrinaire and likely to 'slant' his work in order to convey his religious or more often his political views. The word usefully acts as a warning. Suspicions are natural. It is not the kind of epithet which one expects to find in poetry but it appears in Richard Lovelace's *Lines to Althea from Prison*. One of his couplets,

> Stone walls do not a prison make,
> Nor iron bars a cage,

is known to all, but very few could name the writer.

When Lovelace had described as a happy liberty his entanglement in his darling's hair he went on to declare a cavalier's loyalty to the Crown:

When, like committed linnets, I
    With shriller throat shall sing
The sweetness, mercy, majesty,
    And glories of my king.

The bird was not pledged to a cause; it was put
behind wire bars and still wickedly may be. William Blake might have described his 'robin red-
breast in a cage' as committed.

Comminatory

After a series of electoral victories for the Labour
Party I read in my paper that, in the opinion of
its Political Correspondent, the Conservatives regarded the result as serious but 'not comminatory'.
This puzzled me. It also exposed my ignorance of
the liturgy and practices of the Anglican Church.
I had forgotten its Commination Service, 'a recital
of Divine threatenings against sinners, part of an
office appointed to be read in the Church of England on Ash Wednesday and at other times'. Not
being a regular worshipper paying due attention
to the Lenten ceremonies I do not know whether
this comprehensive damning and blasting is always
and everywhere kept up by minatory clergy and
wonder how it can be combined with the Christian
spirit of forgiveness. In the language of politics
I suppose that a non-comminatory defeat means
that it is not regarded as fatal to future prospects.
There has been a sad day for the losing party but
it has not been consigned to perdition for all time.
    As an example of comminatory conversation
I remember an incident in Copenhagen. On coming
out into the street one night I heard a noisy

outburst of English oaths with a full range of obsceni-
ties and profanities. I said to a Danish friend that
I was sorry to find my countrymen behaving so
shockingly. He said with a laugh that the offenders
were not British. 'They are Danes and Icelanders
and they hate each other so much that they will
not speak or quarrel in their own languages. So
they damn each other in English.' Obviously there
is no lack of linguistic versatility in the harbours
of these contentious nations.

Courtesy

In the surly society of today courtesy is uncommon
both as a practice and as a word. Now rarely met, it
brings a delight of sound appropriate to its gracious
meaning.

> Of Courtesy, it is much less
> Than courage of heart or holiness,
> But in my walks it seems to me
> The Grace of God is in courtesy.

I have never shared Hilaire Belloc's theology, but
I find ample pleasure in his praise of gentle conduct and his choice of language for a lyric.
    In a levellers' world the adjective courteous is
obviously out of place since the Oxford definition
begins 'Having such manners as befit the court of a
prince'. (Why not of a king and a queen?) Then it
moves on to 'gracefully polite and respectful in
dealing with others'. The noun courtesy is not
limited to good manners. It was also a legal term
for 'the form of tenure by which a husband, after
his wife's death, holds certain kinds of property

which she has inherited'. There is an acquisitive spirit about this kind of courtesy which can hardly be called gracious. But the word in its general usage has survived this suggestion of a tight masculine fist. In a shortened form, as the physical salute of a curtsey, it has preserved its quality. Those who want us to be all on the level can hardly have much liking for the lowering of the head and the willingness to 'crook the pregnant hinges of the knee', as Hamlet described the crouch of obeisance. But now the curtsey is curtailed in its extent of humility. The bob respectful has replaced the bow reverential.

Shakespeare included many rare words and curious remarks in that problem child among the large family of his Folio, *Troilus and Cressida*. Very odd indeed are the lines spoken by Ulysses when he is told that Patroclus is present without Achilles for company:

The elephant hath joints, but none for courtesy;
His legs are legs for necessity, not for flexure.

Why this irrelevant piece of zoological information? Certainly it indicates that the elephants in Elizabethan London had no circus tricks. They did not crook the knee as they are sometimes trained to do in a modern circus where there is no equalitarian levelling among the performing animals and flexure is admired in the greater quadrupeds. Camels, whose legs are also necessary for long and burdensome journeys, are seen at times to be capable of courteous flexure.

For some reason which I do not understand courtesy has been given its place in the paint-box. The old authors frequently wrote of the 'pink of courtesy'. Pink, not scarlet. Those whose politics are red may dislike even more the product of the courts of princes.

Credible

To senior readers and listeners it seems astonishing that the idea of belief has vanished from this now frequently employed adjective. We used to talk of a credible story. I have just seen mention of 'a credible military force'. This did not imply that here was an army in whose existence one could believe. Nobody was doubting its presence. Somebody was asserting its strength and utility. Politicians talk of a credible policy when they mean that it is practical. The credibility of a statesman no longer means that he is capable of telling the truth and is not always a liar. It is an intimation that his position in his party is a strong one.

Is it pedantic perfectionism to suggest that the word should be used with a proper understanding that the Latin *credo* means, I believe, not I approve? The sporting journalists have now followed the vogue. I read that a batsman's innings on a cricket field was credible. Creditable would have made sense, but the third syllable has dropped out of the adjective. In suggesting that it be restored, am I being a fuss-pot?

Croodle

In a Victorian novel I read of a young lady who 'clung and croodled' during a respectably amorous session with her gentleman friend. The verb, now I suppose rare if not extinct, is given by Oxford the dignity of dictionary acceptance. Fear seems to have preceded affection, since the first definition is 'to cower, to crouch down'. Then came escape from timidity: 'to draw oneself together, as for warmth, to nestle'. After that another self could share the fireside session. Sex reared its pretty head. Couples croodled.

It is obviously a portmanteau word. Those crouching by the hearth might also cuddle as they croodled. They also could be said to fondle. Making a verb by adding 'le' to a noun or adjective has been a common practice. Cuddle is explained as coming from the old adjective couth which first meant snug or cosy and has been kept pleasantly alive by the Scots in the form couthy. Uncouth ought to mean uncomfortable but has been altered to mean rough or lacking in good manners. One does not think of the Victorian lovers and croodlers as coarse. I imagine them in a drawing-room, not exactly a couthy apartment, but suitable for the maintenance of decorum amid the dalliance.

Canoodle is given a place in the *Penguin Dictionary* where it is defined as 'caress or cuddle'. Eric Partridge describes this as 'American, thoroughly Anglicised by George Augustus Sala in 1864'. This has also been a slang name for a canoe, but that narrow and collapsible vessel is obviously inadequate for amorous voyages. The punt is the safer craft for croodlers.

In the lingo of fondling, caress is the word most pleasing to the ear. Not known to the Elizabethans, it was never used by Shakespeare, but Milton wrote in *Paradise Lost* of high dispute 'solved by conjugal caress'. The Victorian croodling one expects to have been usually a pre-marital form of indulgence.

Defalcate

The vocabulary of crime is a curious mixture. In Shakespeare's England the thieves were curtly and crisply described as nips, foists, prigs and mobs (or mobsmen). They were elevated to being 'light-fingered gentry'. The police of today, with whose procedure and lingo I am constantly acquainted by television programmes, have a completely up-to-date equipment for rapid movement and communication. But they are almost antiquarian when they speak of their administrative areas as manors and parishes and call the law-breakers villains.

For the major financial offences the terminology is, by contrast, ample and imposing. There is the classical Latin and sonorous defalcate which began its life among the trees and in the forester's wood-shed. It meant to cut down or lop off. Then it was used for any form of curtailment or reduction. Thus levelled English could be called defalcated. There could also be defalcation of moral standards with resulting misconduct. Last came the limitation to money matters, particularly to 'the misappropriation of property held on trust'. An alternative is embezzlement, another verbal promotion for swindling.

The Elizabethans called heavy drinkers bezzlers. This suggests a link with booze, originally bouse, but Falstaff and his cronies, hearty bezzlers, were not boozers: that word only arrived in the eighteenth century.

Embezzle seems to be derived from the Latin verb *imbecillare*, meaning to weaken or lay waste. At first there was no connection with villainous peculation. Burton wrote of a spendthrift who embezzled his estate. There was a downward slide into deliberate peculation and defalcation. The crooks have been given classical honours in the names of their crimes. There have been the nouns abactor and abaction specially applied to a cattle-thief and his activities. He could later be charged with the offences of ablation and sequestration. The nips have risen and become enlarged in the verbal environment.

The crime of kidnapping has recently been extensively practised. The kid part of the word was first a boy or girl snatched for sale in the slave-market of the Western plantations. The napping of today has included, sometimes for political reasons, elder persons of money and importance. Even inhabitants of embassies are at risk. There is no diplomatic immunity when the grabbers are on the pounce, but the name of the crime still absurdly suggests that the victims are children. We need a new label when huge sums are demanded to save the life of a senior citizen.

Discrimination

'A man of great discrimination.' It was high praise for one with good judgment and shrewd in his valuation of people and things. Now to discriminate has become a damaging and even dangerous verb. It could lead to a prosecution in a court of law.

The social levellers have had their way. The sexes increasingly look alike and, say many of the women, they must be treated alike. The colours of our skins may vary but there must be no difference in our attitude to mankind's racial differences. To discriminate in that field is a chargeable offence.

Fair enough, but some of the zealots for similarity are carrying their ideas of equality rather far. The height of absurdity was reached when a devotee of porridge advertised for a Scottish cook since he believed that his taste would be better served by a member of that nation whose staple fare it once was and to some extent still is. 'The halesome parritch, chief of Scotia's food,' said Robert Burns in 'The Cotter's Saturday Night'. That is now unlikely to be an occasion for its festive consumption. But it is reasonable that a fancier of the oatmeal should prefer its preparation by one accustomed to a Caledonian kitchen. To ask for one so trained was attacked as wicked discrimination. Why should he not welcome an Oriental in his kitchen? Presumably if a lover of curry had sought for an Indian in his home he would have been no less guilty. Discrimination again! The word has its criminal suggestion.

In the same way distinction might be vetoed as a word of praise since the whole idea of separation and superiority is resented. But there are strange confusions and contradictions here. While the principle of all alike is taken as excellent in some fields, in others there is an unfailing delight in difference of quality and performance. The love of a gamble is a public passion as the vast number of betting shops and their patrons show. The equality of men and women is held to be desirable. But the inequality of horses is their chief attraction in the eyes of the myriads of punters. Do they not discriminate when they place a bet?

Handing out prizes to 'the best of the year' performers on the stage and screen is welcomed by the public as well as by the receivers. There is also great excitement about the selection of the most beautiful women by a panel of supposed experts in the assessment of faces and figures. There can be no levelling of the lovelies in these competitive displays. Discrimination could not be more drastic. But elsewhere to draw distinctions and to make separations is vicious. There must be no 'free choice' when a cook is being selected as likely to make the best of broth or of brose. Best? Must that word has a nasty smell? Yet when I turn on my television set I am confronted with a 'top of the charts' feature called 'Top of the Pops'. The discriminating title is no affront to our new equalitarians.

Drug

A druggist has been a respected name for the owner of a chemist's shop. I see the word now applied to a drug-addict, which is hard on the pharmacist. A drug in the market is no longer a synonym for something too common to be saleable. It is an illicit joy to be obtained in the black market. The customers abound. To be living outside the law with severe penalties for detection as a 'pusher' or consumer of the forbidden article seems not to be an effective deterrent.

The most common traffic is in the product of hemp called cannabis and widely known as pot. As a form of leveller's English this fits the sordid fashion. The adjective cannabine, 'of or pertaining to hemp', has a place in the *O.E.D.* I have never met it in reading or conversation. It has sufficient dignity to make it worthy of a place in the traditional kind of poetry. Such a line as

Consoling herbs and comforts cannabine

is almost Tennysonian. Pottish pleasure would be a meagre substitute.

The sedatives and anodynes have had melody in their names. Shakespeare's 'Poppy nor mandragora, nor all the drowsy syrups of the world' are persuasively soporific. There is a smooth suavity in the name of veronal. It has been suggested that its origin lies in Shakespeare's Verona where Juliet drugged herself with the 'vial of distilled liquor' provided by Friar Laurence and then fell into the 'cold and drowsy humour' which had such disastrous results. Mention of distillation brings to mind the Distillers' Company whose disastrous sale of thalidomide led to calamity in the afflicted homes. Veronal is crystalline, a powder not a potion. According to Oxford it has a hypnotic effect. In the *Penguin Dictionary* it is a 'sedative barbiturate'. Whether mesmeric or soporific, the well-intended gift to Juliet caused a trance of tragic intensity.

The barbiturate drugs, 'a class of organic compounds derived from barbituric acid', are often in the news since an overdose can be fatal and may be suicidally used. Being so close to barbarism the word has a grim look. Curiously a barbiton once suggested dulcet music in the air. It was a sixteenth-century name for a lute or lyre.

It is wrong that dangerous things should have appealing names. There is heroin, for example, a far too encouraging label for one of the 'hard' drugs from whose grip it is very difficult to escape. Morphia soothingly suggests a gift of Morpheus, the classical God of sleep and bringer of dreams, seemingly beneficent but potentially perilous. The general term anaesthetic has, like cannabis and cannabine, a sufficiently harmonious sound and rhythm to find its place in poetry.

Life is the anaesthetic of the soul.

That concluding line of a sonnet came from G. D. H. Cole, the eminent Oxonian Socialist who in his young days was a lyricist and sonneteer before he moved on to be Labour historian, propagandist and writer of detective stories. That was at a time when printing and publication were so cheap that undergraduates could issue their own writings at moderate cost for sale at a shilling or two. They were not always taken seriously. I remember some smiles at this sad dismissal of life as a chloroform. Certainly the statement was not justified in the subsequent career of the dynamic Cole which was as far as could be from a silent coma.

Among the emollients which ease the journey on a trolley carrying a patient to his operation there are anaesthetic injections which have agreeable names. There is methedrin which, in my own experience of the trolley, gives one a delightful 'lift' as the drug-takers call it. One is swept away with all anxiety blissfully dispelled.

The pot-smokers and other druggists do not bother about the vocabulary of their indulgence. A fix, a jab, or a shot suffice for them.

Dudgeon

Macbeth, faced with his real or imagined dagger, saw

On thy blade and dudgeon gouts of blood.

A dudgeon was a wooden handle of a knife. Shakespeare never used the word in its now familiar sense of displeasure and vexation. It was not in Lady Macbeth's language of rebuke when she was chiding her man for his reluctance to be a murderer and a regicide. Yet meaning resentment or disgust, it was in use before she first took the stage. Now, usually carrying the adjective high, it is unlikely to be heard in ordinary conversation despite the suitability of its sound to the sulk. It has become a period word like choleric or mumpish, which have vanished. When the boss or Big Noise at the works or the office is snapping and snarling it is most unlikely that any of his underlings would warn his companions about high dudgeon mumpish in the air.

There might be mention of a sore head or of a tantrum, which belongs to the 'origin obscure' class. There was a slightly longer form of this, tantarem, which meant a loud and presumably choleric shouting. Among the senior names for sulk umbrage, given or taken, is still heard. It meant shade and the adjective umbrageous was properly used of woods and forests. At first 'a man in umbrage' was a man under suspicion. Then the idea of indignation came in.

The contemporary alternatives are not impressive. The growling, once gnarling, boss is said to be in a stew or a pet or cutting up rough. We might possibly hear of a paddy-whack, shortened to paddy, for an irascible outburst of temper, but on the whole brevity has prevailed.

An exception to this levelling down must be admitted in the case of disgruntle, which Oxford accepts as an active verb meaning 'to put into ill humour or chagrin'. The passive past participle disgruntled is more commonly met. It is a word of modern invention based on the idea of angry grunting and now applied to any kind of dissatisfaction. One rarely hears gruntle for grumble or gruntled for annoyed, but they have their place in the dictionary.

To be disgruntled is not to be distraught. It

46

brings to mind a mild form of peevishness with no violent display of choler or paddy. Peevish, another 'origin unknown' adjective, was a favourite of Shakespeare's in whose plays there are peevish characters. Linked with it was froward, described as 'not now in colloquial use'. Froward or refractory brats have become known as difficult, which is less censorious, or problem children, which also excuses their bad conduct and suggests that the traditional reward of 'a good slap' is a barbarous relic of an age which had never heard of the psychological treatment suggested by up-to-date magistrates as the answer to young turbulence and violence. These are now given the evasive name of juvenile delinquency. I am tired of delinquency. As a cover for inexcusable conduct which it would be reactionary to punish, it rouses my own dudgeon. One thing that our permissive age will not forgive is the old and simple habit of calling sin sin. Yet the levellers, with their addiction to the single syllable, should be fond of that.

Dumps and Domp

In his book *Need Your Doctor be so Useless?* Dr Andrew Malleson points out that some cures expected to alleviate are likely to aggravate. The treatment or prescription, he maintains, may induce one trouble while seeking to allay another. In his own words 'diseases and their activities that are caused by doctors are called Iatrogenic'. Sometimes they are just called Domp, which stands for 'Diseases of Medical Practice'. 'Domp', he adds, 'is now common.'

During a long life in which I have owed much to the technical skill of the master-cutlers in the

Operating Theatre and to the good sense of some, not all, general practitioners, I may sometimes have been iatrogenically domped. To this it may be replied that I have none the less survived beyond normal expectation. One reason for my luck may be a comatose nature. I have not so far been compelled to drug myself in order to sleep. The discontented young, rejecting the discipline and drudgery of a settled career, are said to 'drop out'. I have been an easy 'dropper-off', which was a comfort at night but a plague in the afternoons when there was work to do. So on my bedside table there is not a large collection of the pills packed in similar tubes and often inadequately labelled. This reduces the risk of mistakes and of what Dr Malleson politely calls 'adverse drug-reaction'.

The chances of a domp are multiplied as much by the lavishness of prescription as by the negligence of the insistent pill-addicts. Dr Malleson discovered that 'for only 15 per cent of 300 consecutive patients seen by me in a London general practice was it acceptable to prescribe a drug. Actually I found it impossible to reduce my prescribing rate as low as this for that would have caused a waiting-room rebellion.' Was he weak to surrender? Doctors are nearly always over-worked. They have no time for coping with protest demonstrations in consulting rooms and for listening to the indignant eloquence of pill-craving people who are in 'the dumps' and angrily claiming to be deprived if a dose be denied.

The ordinary patient will not tolerate any refusal of medication. Has he not paid for the National Health Service? Pay and get no pill or potion? That would be robbery. Hence the popularity of the tablet or draught called a 'placebo'. The pleasant relief which that word implies may be absent. There may also be harm done by iatrogenic domp. But there is the joyful awareness that at least something therapeutic has been done. Since we are all so beset by long classical words in and out of the sick-room, that happy condition must now be called euphoric.

Ecodoomster

Ecology, 'a study of the relations of living organisations to their environment', has become a word of frequent appearance. That is natural since, being ourselves living organisations, we have every reason to worry about our surroundings, now called our environmental condition. Environment has been promoted to the naming of one of the most important ministries in Whitehall. There the ecologists are consulted about the perils confronting all land-animals, including ourselves, the birds and the fish in the polluted seas.

I have seen the title of Ecodoomster applied to one of the scientific forecasters of our destiny who was taking a dim and indeed doomful view of our future. There will soon, as we are told, be far too many people with far too little to eat. The affliction of famine is likely to spread from the under-nourished races to our still fairly well-nourished selves. If that is so, among the doomed will be those prolific writers of the Good Food Guides who prattle on about the luxurious meals which they may get for nothing from the owner of the restaurants and which the ordinary man calls 'posh nosh'. If the ecodoomsters are correct there is chance of survival only for authors of books and articles on 'Some Grub, if any, and where to find it'. They may tell us that 'at Chow's', the popular rendezvous of the tuck-hunters in Soho, you can get the best bowl of rice, garnished with a boiled potato, that London can offer'. Fortunately there are more cheerful prophets who say that the ecodoom theorists have been overdoing it and that a few millionaire gourmets may still be able to fuss over a sumptuous salmi while the millions of common folk are just making do with their meagre ration of nutritional units. These may be relieved by an occasional feast of baked beans or fish fingers, assuming that sewage and chemical seepage, of which the doomsters have much to say, have not made all sea-foods poisonous. We have our optimists who assure us that the dietary Doomsday is another day, possibly the day after tomorrow.

Turning from eatables to etymology we can find some satisfaction in our vocabulary of despair. Doom—short, dark and menacing—is a word perfectly suited to its purpose. It did not always imply disaster. It began as a statute or law, probably harsh and possibly equitable. King Alfred's England had its Doombook, a code of laws. Better known is William the Conqueror's Domesday Book, 'a record of the Great Inquisition or Survey of the lands of England, their extent, value, ownership and liabilities'. The historian Matthew Paris praised the justice of its accounting and then, somewhat morosely, explained its title: 'It judgeth all as the Lord on the Great Day will do.'

Doom has been a grand asset to the admonitory preachers and the poets telling tales of woe. It comes rolling out in the sermons of John Donne, the gloomiest of gloomy Deans. For the rhymers in tragic or macabre mood it has usefully served as their unhappy characters proceed from womb to tomb, while catastrophe looms. Now it can be linked with the zoom of bomb-carrying aeroplanes. In compound words it rings the funeral bell. Doom-burdened is a sonorous example of

that. So we survive, until the crack of doom, pre-
cariously as the ecodoomsters say.

Explosion

One cannot read a page in a newspaper without
meeting another detonation. Some unfortunate
people cannot pick up an envelope delivered by
post without fearing a lethal bang. Blasting by
gelignite is the common practice of the numerous
Angry Brigades and other gunpowder plotters. Employed in metaphor the bangs are incessant. Population does not grow too fast and spread too far. It
explodes. So does language. So do communicators.
The subject of an article on my desk is 'linguistic
science' and the contribution made to it by an
American Professor, Dr Naom Chomsky, 'whose
status as a revolutionary is assured in this field.'
'He has been compared to Copernicus', and pre-
Chomskyan linguistics are informally dubbed 'linguistics B.C.'. We are further told that 'linguistics,
the scientific study of human language, as an
autonomous system, has been going through a remarkable growth period in the last decade or so,
propelled by the communications explosion from
the periphery to the centre of attention of the
human sciences'. A principal reason for this has
been the work of Naom Chomsky who in 1957, before he was thirty, published the first version of
his revolutionary linguistic theories which have
come to be called transformational-generative, in
an elegant volume called *Syntactic Structures*. The
elegance achieved by the author and publisher is
not accompanied by similar grace in the explana-
tory style of his admiring expositor, who is a University librarian.

I am puzzled by the double-barrelled adjective applied to the Chomskyan wisdom. Transformational-generative suggests to me an elaborate piece of electric equipment more than the study of words and their use which is what interests my unscientific self. But one thing is certain. Chomsky has dropped a bomb of record size and potency in the once quiet territory of the English or Anglo-American language. Will the science of linguistics continue to explode? It will be in the fashion if it does. I note that transformational-generative is now so familiar an adjective that it is called by its fanciers 'T.G.'. Here is verbal levelling, and that in an unexpected place.

Extrapolation and Tripos

Some diminish our language. A few enlarge it with long and cumbrous innovations. The latter, who may be called longitudinarians, are usually in the academic centres. I was reminded of this by reading a letter in *The Times* on the subject of the rejected plans for vehicles known as Hovertrains. It began

> Sir, Extrapolations from our present position indicate that in five to ten years we shall be faced with a transport crisis which will make the present discomfort, pollution and muddle seem almost efficient. The results so far from the Hovertrain research suggest that it could be one of the most useful, ecologically and economically, projects ever sponsored.

This came from Cambridge, which wins by its proficiency in the Higher Mathematics a similar esteem to that of Oxford's lexicography. From the former came a use of the word extrapolation which sent me to the latter for clarification. I learned that to extrapolate has nothing to do with escape or removal from Arctic or Antarctic zones, as well it might. It is 'to fill in values or terms of a series on either side of the known values or to continue a curve beyond the points for which the data have been obtained'. My ignorance got small relief from that. But after this definition, marked in a bracket as 'math', there came the information, bracketed as 'fig', that to extrapolate is also 'to argue from the known to the unknown, to infer'. If 'reckon' is meant, why not say so in two syllables? Here I am a leveller and will not extrapolate. The mathematicians can keep that. Am I then wrangling with a Wrangler? The strange use of that name for one who has taken a First Class in the Cambridge Mathematical Tripos suggests that he is likely to be quick and powerful in contention. I have been warned of his pugnacity, but am still puzzled.

Why Tripos? Do the examinees sit perched painfully on tripods, three-legged stools? I turn from the Cam to the Thames for enlightenment. Once the would-be Wranglers were physically as well as mentally racked when they squatted for their degrees. This Tripos has a curious history. Originally it meant a person, not a perch. Oxford defines the word as 'a bachelor of arts who was appointed to dispute in a humorous or satirical style with the candidates for degrees at "Commencement", so called from the three-legged stool on which he sat'. He had to keep his sense of merriment as well as his balance while engaged in his disputation. A Tripos was also 'a set of humorous verses composed by a human Tripos'. So 'to be good at sums' (levellers' English) once required mastery of the lighter Muse in addition to bodily poise and knowledge of mathematics in depth.

C. S. Calverley, who attended and rhymed at both the old universities, would have made an admirable Tripod man, as far as the literary talent was concerned. Cambridge made exacting and extensive demands, but those requirements and some of their vocabulary seem to have been abandoned in 1894. The Wranglers, no longer wrangling, remain. In recounting, and under correction explaining, the tale of the Tripods and Triposes I may be said to extrapolate. But up with that word I will not put.

Fan

The fanciers of a theatrical personality or a 'pop singer' have been reduced to fans. Some literary journalists avoid that levelling and show their linguistic range by writing of afficionados. I think devotees will do. It is some time since Beatle-mania raged and even rioted. Recently there have been swarms of juvenile and female Cassidy fans who beset that minstrel with hysterical screams of admiration. They are called in the press reports of their uproar and physical contortions 'teeny-boppers'. Teenagers they mostly are, but why this bopping? I have seen the alternative form, 'weeny-boppers'. In neither case do I think we have an invention worth retaining.

At one time fans were frequently paid to provide newsworthy applause. They had the French name of *claque*. Now there is no need for hire and salary in such tributes. The boppers appear to be in funds since they are ready to make long journeys at some cost in order to howl round an arriving aeroplane at Heathrow. What do the letters BOP stand for? In my boyhood they indicated the *Boys' Own Paper*, a pious publication which mingled fiction with ethical advice. Barmy on Pop? It may be so.

Fanfaronade

Britain's entry into the European Common Market at the beginning of 1973 was celebrated with what the promoters called a Fanfare. That word properly means a salute with a blast of the powerful brass provided by trumpeters, a noise once known as a tucket. This augustly arranged welcome to a political and economic move not widely popular here included music of the highest quality. If the flow of harmony was supposed to be symbolic of enduring love among the co-operating nations it was optimistic. Fanfare seemed an odd label. The trumpet's note is more often martial than amorous and affectionate.

In describing the cultural programme with dutiful enthusiasm one journalist amplified the title and wrote of a Fanfaronade. By adding the two extra syllables he was being complimentary, but inaccurate. The fanfaronade was rhetorical not musical. It was a torrent of boisterous boasting, usually a solo turn and by no means orchestral. He who delivered it was not joining in a demonstration of communal goodwill. He spoke for his own self of which he had a very good opinion. In doing so he was 'spuming the High Froth', as H. G. Wells's Mr Polly put it.

The nations have had a variety of names for the verbal ebullience of the Frothers. In Urquhart's translation of Rabelais the cascades of vainglorious magniloquence are listed as 'The Gasconads of

France, the Fanfaronads of Italy and the Rodo-
montads of Spain'. I like the sound of this notable
foreign company to which we have added the final
e's. Urquhart was wrong in his attributions of
locality. (I am using a lot of long words, but that
is surely right for the subject.) Rodomontade owes
its origin to a character in the epic *Orlando Furioso*
written by Ariosto of Ferrara, whose Rodomont
was a master of the fanfaronade.

It is worth note that after the Renaissance there
was a great delight in large, new words, portentous,
picturesque, and as plentiful in number as in
syllables. The loquacity became ludicrous and was
mocked by the writers of comedies who were constantly getting fun out of the fashionable froth.
Here was the reverse of linguistic levelling. In the
writing and satirical comedy of today there are
no successors to the characters once mocked for
their verbal exhibitionism. In modern plays the
dialogue is mainly a click-clack of muttered monosyllables. From time to time John Osborne, who
is not ashamed of owning an ample vocabulary,
allows some angry fellow to deliver a tirade. Otherwise there is a complete absence of froth, high or
low. The actors employ the 'throw-away' method as
they patter out their possibly witty but usually
jejune lines. There are no Rodomonts for derision. The ears of the audience are starved. A fanfaronade, whether abusive or boastful, would be
an unexpected pleasure.

Farrago and Fascicule

A farrago was originally 'mixed fodder for cattle'.
It became the bundle in which it was collected.
Fascicule was an alternative. (The title of Fascist

came from the ancient Roman bundle of disciplinary rods.) Because farrago was born in the cowshed it has rarely if ever been employed in the giving of praise. A review of the kind of book known as a miscellany would not describe it as 'a farrago of excellent opinions excellently expressed'. One meets instead a 'farrago of trash'. But in that case the trashy book would be different.

That word also comes from the rejects in food preparation. Trash was the refuse of the sugar-cane after the juice had been pressed out. Our terms of disparagement draw much from the farmyard. A small payment is chicken-feed. The commonest fascicule now is 'a load of old rubbish'. Why always old rubbish? Is bosh never new? Is trash never trendy, to use an adjective now in use?

I read and hear many an up-to-date farrago of fatuity. An ancient lumping together of bits and pieces from the larder was a gallimaufry. Using up the remains of a recent meal has added simple native variants, such as hodge-podge and mishmash. The 'left-overs' rescued to be highly spiced for a lordly table became a salmagundi. The look and sound of that are impressive but somewhat alarming. There may be windy weather to follow, but that is a risk with all farraginous and fasciculate concoctions. As an economical form of food-salvage there is a compound dish called 'resurrection pie'. That I discovered in a crossword puzzle. In my family the pie was attributed to shepherds. That, suggesting pastures not bone-yards, is surely preferable for the thrifty use of remainders which need not be insipid if flavouring has been skilfully injected into the farrago.

Feed-back

This word is now used for answer or reply, presumably to give an air of scientific precision. It is defined as 'a system of diverting out-going current to strengthen in-coming current'. The prevailing taste for the jargon of the technocrats has carried the word into unlikely places. One of those is the vocabulary of the trade unionists. A shop-steward, when questioned about the likelihood of a strike, was reported as saying that the officials had put the matter to the members but had not yet received their feed-back. I notice the term frequently employed when there is a discussion of a popular reaction to a suggested policy. Such an inquiry has now to be called a questionnaire. When one of these frequently dispatched documents arrives on my desk I either tear it up as involving a silly waste of time or trouble or give it an answer. Not being an electrician I do not feed back the requested facts and opinions.

Fridge

It has become one of the commonest words in household use. It would indeed be surprising to hear a domestic order to 'put it in the refrigerator'. When various Governments imposed, or attempted to impose, a rigidly frigid control of wages and prices in 1973, the English-speaking nations were faithful to the monosyllabic freeze, without a slide into slang. There was no fridge in Whitehall. If the politicians and economists had been aware of the vocabulary at their disposal, they could not only have refrigerated and infrigerated the economy but also have glaciated, congelated and conglaciated our finances. Sensibly they spared us that lingo.

Shakespeare's choice of an adjective when he wrote of death as the soul's exile in 'thrilling region of thick-ribbed ice' reminds us that thrill was once a powerful and frightening word. Since his time it has been so overworked that it now suggests only a minor excitement and an inconsiderable shiver. Consequently the hard-worked super has been brought to its rescue. Films are advertised as containing 'a thousand super-thrills'. Is the horror-hungry public the more attracted? Super should be given a rest.

By an odd accident similar words beginning with 'fr' and including 'z' have been applied to extremes of both heat and cold. Things frizzle in the frying-pan. The bodies of nudists may be said to frizzle if they practise their exposure in very hot climates. The London bathers who fancy a dip in the Serpentine on Christmas morning come near to freezing. Yet if there has been a hard frost they may encounter a frazil which happens to mean 'a piece of granular or spiky ice'. A frazzle suggests kinship with a frizzle, but the noun comes from the verb to fray and means an exhausted condition. Defeated and distraught persons are said to be 'beaten to a frazzle'. They may as the result be spoken of as hot and bothered, but that is incidental. Efforts to impose a freeze on wages had a chilly reception and reduced some politicians to a frazzle.

Gab

If the remark that jaw-jaw is better than war-war is rightly attributed to Sir Winston Churchill he was coming down to levelled language from the verbal altitudes on which he had once been a mountaineer. In a speech delivered in the House of Commons in February 1906 on the subject of indentured Chinese labour in South Africa, which his party, then the Liberals, had vehemently denounced as slavery during the recent General Election, he met the Conservative accusation that they had been lying with the following words which, since prolixity is involved, deserve to be called a 'pronouncement':

> In the opinion of His Majesty's Government it cannot be classified as slavery in the extreme acceptance of that word without some risk of terminological inexactitude.

His remark was a smooth, ingenious and entertaining reply to an acrimonious attack. In it he wittily substituted eleven syllables for one.

Cutting out the long words in his war-time broadcasts to the nation, he could at any time turn from the economical to the verbally prodigal style. A notable example of that occurred in his little book on the comfort of painting as a relief from boredom for the elderly. Old age he accurately described as 'the surly advance of decrepitude'.

Sometimes using a few words as what actors call 'punch-lines' and sometimes using many in a no less memorable way, he demonstrated that he had what is often called 'the gift of the gab' and indeed of two gabs. The first use of that phrase I cannot discover. It may be ranked as slang but, by including it in his 'treasury of English words', somewhat forbiddingly described as 'a Thesaurus', Peter Mark Roget (1779–1869), or his son, who enlarged his work, recognised it as something properly acceptable. It is put side by side with such solemn terms as locution, parlance and prolation, none of which I care for. Parlance is frequently linked with the adjective common. I feel more at home with gab. Prolation, for spouting, did not survive the eighteenth century.

Here one meets some curious company. For the opposite of the gab-gift Roget has 'aphony, obmutescence and vacuity'. These limitations to eloquence were certainly not Churchillian. Winston aphonous! When he was brief? Absurd idea! It is an adjective which Roget mentioned as a synonym for dumb, muzzled and mum.

The last of these has had some strange additions. Charles Lamb wrote of an aphonous man as 'sitting mumchance'. Before him 'Hudibras' Butler had used the puzzling word mum-budget for a gabless fellow.

Gabby as an adjective came in, I think, from America. James Agate, in reviewing a transatlantic musical show, called talkative young ladies 'gabby dolls', which was right for the vocabulary and dialogue of the piece in question. Then, turning to a Shakespearian performance, he observed that some of the Bard's feminine and by no means mumchance characters qualified for that description of those 'dolls' who may be charged with mental vacuity but not with oral obmutescence.

Gamboge and Magenta

Part of the levelling process has been a thinning out of our colour-names. Except in horticultural catalogues and books by gardening specialists, we make do with the reds, blues, yellows and blacks and forget the old and ample variations. I was reminded of this by encountering gamboge in a crossword puzzle. This recalled my first schoolboy's paint-box. I was fascinated by the livid yellow of the tablet marked gamboge. The word was a nice sticky one and quite a mouthful since it had to be pronounced gambooge. As a mouthful of another kind this product of gum-resin would have been troublesome. A section of paint, a child was told, is not for eating, however much it resembles a caramel. In this case consumption would have been painfully punished since gamboge is further described by Oxford as 'a drastic purge'. Did doctors ever prescribe it in cases of severe constipation?

Its companion yellow is the chrome of a mineral found in many countries. Mixed with lead sulphate it offers artists a selection of tints. There are chrome red and chrome orange as well as the more familiar yellow.

Another curious colour-name is magenta, the product of a crimson aniline dye. Why was it so called? Apparently because it was discovered in 1859 shortly after the battle of Magenta in Lombardy, where a mixed army of French and Sardinians defeated the Austrian invaders. Oxford's connection of the hue with the conflict is curious. The town had a silk industry in which presumably the fabric was richly coloured with the dye. Like the queer gamboge the pleasant word magenta is not often used now. It might be more enjoyed to bedizen our vocabulary.

The English male of the hearty, non-foppish type is apt to go capriciously gay about the neck. The Old School Tie has survived some derision and its blend of colours is frequently of a dazzling kind. There may be some college whose OBs sport a blend of gamboge and magenta round their throats. I belong to a club whose distinguishing neckerchief is almost as flamboyant as that, but I refrain from wearing anything so gambogious. That adjective has its place in the dictionaries.

Gazump

During the grotesque boom in the prices of land and houses which occurred recently this no less grotesque word arrived to describe a rise in price demanded after a property had been put on the market for a specified sum. Eric Partridge includes Gezumpher, a Yiddish slang word for a swindler which later became Gazumper. It came in as slang but was given legal status by a Judge who was examining this kind of financial pressure. With Gazump also in use it was obvious that King Lear's dismissal of 'zed' as an 'unnecessary letter' did not apply to the language of the year as spoken in Courts of Justice, political assemblies and auction-rooms.

I notice that one of the house-and-garden properties whose price has soared contained a gazebo, 'a turret or summer-house from which to enjoy the adjacent scenic amenities'. A gazebo sounds most consonant with the activities of a gazumper.

Ghetto and Others

There is now much muddled use of this word, which is a shortened form of the Italian *borghetto*, meaning a small part of a town. At first there was no specification of its inhabitants, but it came to be specially applied to a district set apart for Jews when these people were segregated and treated as outcasts. The first use of the word was in 1608. It was never in Shakespeare's vocabulary. One would expect to find it in *The Merchant of Venice*, but that was written round about 1595. If there was a Jewish *borghetto* in Venice Shylock was not confined to it. He could do business on the Rialto at risk of insult, but he did so successfully, and his home, from which his daughter Jessica fled, seems not to have been a shabby one in a despised location.

Ghetto frequently occurs now in English. Sometimes it is applied to run-down areas. The reports of the recurring riots in Belfast in 1973 spoke of shooting and looting in a Roman Catholic or Protestant ghetto. This the reader or listener took to be one of the drab sections of the town. There was no suggestion of a Northern Irish Jewry. The members of that race have too much sense to stay amid the racial hatreds of the savagely contentious Christians.

In England the ghetto has become an enclave for a special type of person who may be a native Londoner. When the Labour Party in the borough of Camden was planning drastic rehousing in the district known as Gospel Oak there were protests against the destruction of some pleasant and still habitable 'period' houses in order to erect a pile of council flats. The leader of the local Labour

Party retorted, 'We do not want a middle-class ghetto here.'

There was a more striking elevation of the ghetto when there were disputes about the taking over for grandiose development of a majestic mansion on Highgate Hill and the new use of its spacious grounds. Against the proposals of a property-owning company to build expensively it was urged that the space could be better used for comparatively cheap accommodation. Reference to the Department of the Environment evoked a decision that the conservation of a unique site with superb views over Hampstead Heath and London would be better achieved by the allotment of some of the grounds to public use while a few houses of high quality were built on the rest of it. A newspaper comment said that this would turn the coveted spot into 'a plutocrats' ghetto'. The tycoons may come in and some of them may be Jewish but when I read on the same day of the wretched sectarian ghettos in Belfast I decided that our vocabulary for the classification of urban areas needed correction. Ghettos for millionaires as well as for the middle class are absurd.

For an alternative there is purlieu, which came into the language of land-owners and lawyers in the sixteenth century. At first it was limited to the rustic and sylvan. It was a place on the fringe of a forest. Shakespeare used it once and accurately. His purlieu is mentioned in *As You Like It* by Oliver de Boys as part of the Forest of Arden, where Orlando 'gave battle to the lioness' which had so curiously arrived there. With that beast of prey as well as 'a green and gilded snake' on the pounce this purlieu was one to avoid. But in general purlieus could be profitable for those who knew how to seize an opportunity. A purlieu-man was one who established a freehold of land in or beside a forest. If his heirs and descendants held on long enough they had precious property and may now be millionaires. Purlieu would be the right name for the well-timbered mansion on Highgate Hill which was accused of becoming the ghetto of the wealthy.

Against that it may be said that later on purlieus came down in the world and that the name was sometimes attached to mean streets in the poorer suburbs. However I have seen it rescued by an American writer about London who described Hampstead as 'an art and culture purlieu'. It was no slum in that case, whereas many a ghetto has deserved to be so called. Slum is a word of mysterious origin not used until the nineteenth century, and probably made painfully familiar by the feeling that a noun or adjective beginning with 'sl' must be associated with squalour. Slum is a dictionary neighbour to slatterns, slovens, slugs, sluts and the portentously named Slubberdegullions who arrived in the seventeenth century to join the deplorable slum-company of slobs, who are defined as dull, slow, untidy persons.

Gigs, Giglets, and Gigglers

The gig went to sea as a boat. It went on the roads as a light horse-drawn carriage. Carlyle wrote of the gigman as a social type, not of lordly rank but as a substantial member of the carriage-owning class. On a lower level, in both senses of the adjective, it went spinning on the pavement as a child's top. So Shakespeare used it: 'To see great Hercules whipping a gig'. As a verb to gig means to fidget and move to and fro. Did that help to create the name of giglet or giglot who at first could be a servant-girl with no imputation of misconduct? The country towns once had their Giglet Fairs where she went to find an employer. Now the process is reversed. Any housekeeper is delighted to find a maid ready for domestic work. Possibly for lack of a job some of the young women stopped seeking to sell 'one pair of hands' and put other parts of the body on the market. The 'giglot wench', another of Shakespeare's gigs, became a wanton.

The name may have been due to her gigging about the streets or the fairground. Or it can have come from her merriment. Was she a giggler before she was a sinner? 'To laugh continuously in a manner suggestive of foolish levity' is one dictionary's definition of the horrid verb. Its origin is listed as 'echoic'. It is derived, like cackle, from the noise it makes when spoken. It may be that chortle, invented by Lewis Carroll, was also chosen for that reason. They are somewhat repulsive words. Laughter is kinder to exhibitions of mirth, at least to those of moderate glee.

Commonly now an entertainment is said to be 'good for a giggle'. The recommendation does not appeal to me. I rank my brow as one of middling altitude and do not shrink from the dilemmas and disasters of the farcical comedian whose repeated entrances and exits are through bedroom doors and whose expected deprivation is the loss of his trousers. I can share the chortler's joy in this routine, but I refuse to admit that I giggle.

It puzzles me that dramatic critics, whose praise of a 'wow' is seized for quotation in the announcements of plays, so often describe the mirthful members of the audience as 'rolling in the aisles'. I have never seen any of the enraptured picked up from the floor of a theatre gangway by the attendants and restored to his or her seat in no longer prostrate hilarity. Such a removal would be obligatory since, owing to the fire-precautions, the aisles must be clear of all obstructions, even the bodies of those whom the classical scholars call hyper-gelasts, which is Greek for incurable gigglers. If the hyper-gelasts resisted replacement and continued to roll, their stomachs might also earn the adjective gasteropodous which is normally applied to 'molluscs, including snails and limpets, so called from the ventral position of the locomotive organ'. Thus the description of a super-chortle as a belly-laugh is physically relevant.

Hum

The short verb hum usually means 'to make a low continuous murmuring sound or note' and hence, as in humming and hawing, to be either inarticulate or dissatisfied. The other usage, for to cheat or hoax, has dwindled, but lingers on in compounds. We may be swindled. We may be 'conned'. We are unlikely to be hummed. Curiously, a similar term for a species of noise, buzz, used to be a slang word for cheating or robbing. I remember the time when the great Marie Lloyd was singing one of her old songs that never fades away, 'My Old Man said "Follow the Van"'. The homeless, evicted, penniless woman, whom she portrayed with such poignancy, fumbled in her dingy little purse to find the price of a consoling drink, then small enough. There was nothing there. 'Girls,' she said to the audience, 'I've been buzzed.' It was not a comic ditty though now it is often wrongly put across as though it were a riot of fun. With her it was a mean street tragedy, unforgettable in tattered pathos.

She might have said 'I've been hummed'. The idea of deceit was kept in hum-dudgeon, a pretended or imaginary illness. It has become established in humbug, whose attachment to a large sucky sweet is hard to explain. It is no fraud, but a genuinely satisfying mouthful or gob. The other humbug is familiar and for those wishing to enlarge our language and exhibit their range of long words there are impressive variations, cozenage, circumvention, subreption, which is better known in its adjectival form of surreptitious, and ingannation. To use the last two is carrying erudition rather far. Who would understand a grumbler who complained of being subrepted or ingannated? I owe these to Roget and not to hearing them in ordinary conversation or even to any recent reading.

Ours is an age of verbal humbug, especially in politics and sociology. Some of the lingo is partly due to compassion which provides an excuse for it. In my note to come under the title Nut, on the evasive terms for madness or lunacy, I mention the merciful tendency to avoid the old dismissal of the mentally afflicted to Bedlams, loony-bins and asylums. To speak of mental homes is charitable, and the many slang names for those with 'a screw loose' or 'round the bend' are not cruelly intended. What is deplorable is the refusal to use such simple and accurate adjectives as poor and old. Though the purpose is kind, the humbug is tiresome. There is no disgrace in age or poverty. The first is inevitable; the second is often the result of misfortune, not of a foolish, wasteful life. That the poor we have always with us is a plain statement of fact with biblical authority. But now we must say that the under-privileged are a permanent section of the community. This is particularly silly since it is implied that privilege is a good thing which should be equally shared and not an injustice

which should be mitigated or abolished if we believe in equity and fair shares.

So the humbug spreads. Old age must not be
mentioned in the official jargon. The Senior
Citizens have their Retirement Pensions. The
vicious youngsters, the muggers who assault and
even murder in their robberies, are not criminals,
not even scoundrels. They are delinquents. The
luckless victims of unemployment, which in many
cases is a social accident, have to be spoken of as
redundant. I draw my Old Age Pension unashamed.
I am, if you insist, a Senior Citizen. But I should
prefer to be called an old crock and a fogey. I dislike this evasive humming.

The Hydros

The Greek name for water has had a remarkable
fascination for our word-makers. Our native word
for 'the transparent colourless liquid, the normal
oxide of hydrogen' has served the poets in many a
fluent and memorable line, but elsewhere it has been
rejected in favour of long classical formations. Not
only in the sciences is length preferred. During
Scottish holidays I often stayed in hotels equipped
with a variety of baths. Hotels? No; they were
Hydropathic Establishments. They were very
watery places. In most of them there was nothing
else to drink unless one made private arrange-
ments for other liquid comforts and stimulations.
The second part of the title indicated that curative
dips and douches were available. There were, however, consolations for the absence of whisky in its
homeland: fine grounds in noble, mountainous surroundings, tennis, golf, and a hostess to link up
those seeming lonely and to set the couples

dancing. Many of the young then managed to be gay without gin. Round the billiard-room of one Hydro there was an array of lockers in which the less austere elders with a thirst kept their privy store of bottles. The Hydro had its regard for private needs and was quietly permissive.

Close to the Highland Hydros were galloping rivers soon to be cleverly harnessed for economic use. That might have been simply called 'Power from the Glens'. There was no such verbal simplicity. They were Hydro-Electric Schemes or Hydro-Dynamic Developments.

Noël Coward has told us in an often repeated song that 'Mad dogs and Englishmen go out in the mid-day sun'. He was a master of the monosyllable: the diction in the dialogue of his plays is clipped, curt, and compelling, rattling along with the cracks and retorts that are as brief as they are witty. There was no mention of rabies in his lyric about the habits of tropical company. If there had been, it would not have been called hydrophobia, the name usually given to that disease. In fact that word means 'intense fear of water'. The timid, reluctant bather who prefers the sand to the sea and those averse to basins, soaps and towels can accurately be described as hydrophobians. But the medicals took over that label since one of the symptoms of rabies, when man is infected with it, is 'an aversion to liquids and difficulty in swallowing them'.

The hydra in Greek mythology was a huge and many-headed water-snake. Effective decapitation was impossible because its heads grew again as soon as they were cut off. Only Hercules could cope with it. Mention of this poly-cephalic creature brings us back to the land of the Hydropathics. Loch Ness, at least for the persistent believers in a Monster, has some form of Highland Hydra.

So the contempt for the word water continues. We are carried over it in hydro-planes. A water-pipe connecting with a main cannot be simply that. It must be a hydrant. You may have water on the brain. If so, you are hydrocephalic.

Ideology

The lengtheners cannot resist an 'ology'. So the ideas of a person or a party become their ideology. The added syllables are thought to give increased importance to opinions which may not merit that promotion to scientific status. The name of sociology, defined as 'the study of the behaviour of groups', now rides high in the academic world and attracts plentiful students to form their ideologies on what they learn in its lecture-rooms. There were no chairs of sociology in my university years. But those were the bad old days of a narrow curriculum and I was an Oxbridge product. That jumbled place-name word has become so widely used that it appears in the *Penguin Dictionary*, as also does Red-brick, defined as 'a University founded in modern times'. These up-to-date and 'with-it' academies are the swarming grounds of sociologists who organise research into ideologies. When their questionnaires have produced their feed-back they issue reports whose value is itself questionable. The sociological surveys of ideology sound very solemn. So brief a term as 'a quiz about views' would never do. The syllables must multiply. In the lingo I note that people no longer agree with a creed or a cause. They prefer to say that they do or do not identify themselves with this or that ideology. Preferable to the extremes of brevity and prolixity there is a central way. Language is a medium of communication and that word suggests a middle English for the discussion of ideas.

Jargon

It is a characteristic of the general ignorance and carelessness about words in common use that I have often written about 'the lingo' commonly called jargon without wondering about the origin and history of this strange word. As usual when one bothers to do a little research the result is surprising. Coming to us from France it began as a warbling of birds, for which pleasing sound there was the old alternative, charm. Milton wrote of 'morn rising sweet with charm of earliest birds'. Was there ever a poetic salute to the jargon of the nightingale? If so, it has vanished. There also disappeared the melody first implicit in the word. The idea of a warble wilted. The jargon became a tuneless twittering. The sparrows took over from the songsters.

From twittering in the garden there was a move to the human chattering in the house. A modern cocktail party is a jamboree of jargoneers. Oxford gives the date of 1643 to the appearance of jargon as 'a barbarous, rude or debased variety of speech'. Later, as a term of contempt it was applied to 'the language of scholars, the terminology of a science or art or the cant of a class, sect, trade or profession'. That is its present usage and since that kind of cant, defined as the peculiar language of a class, has greatly expanded in our age of scientific invention and technological contrivance, there is a jargon explosion.

Juggernaut

The nuisance of very large lorries or trucks grinding through the narrow streets of very small villages as well as blocking the centres of big towns and traffic-jammed cities has caused juggernaut to appear constantly in the papers, where it may be as often mentioned as is our own bulldozer. The latter is 'a large machine of a caterpillar tractor type used for levelling rough ground or cutting through mounds of earth'. The so-called juggernaut uses and damages roads already made. The name has appealed because of its monstrous and aggressive appearance. It is misused when it is implied that it is a menace to shrinking pedestrians who are evading it to save their lives. The original Indian juggernaut was large but only lethal for those eager to be immolated. It began as a title of the divine Hindu Krishna, the eighth avatar of Vishnu. (An avatar is the appearance of a god on earth in corporal form.) The huge vehicle called a juggernaut was not carrying goods to market or materials to a factory. It was loaded with a vast image of the god dragged once a year in procession through a city in Orissa. The worshippers instead of standing in veneration lay down in their devotion in order to be crushed to death.

Lecture and Teach-in

Lectures have been levelled to teach-ins, a recent vogue word which has been given headline status in *The Times*. At school and college I had been taught in classes and attended lectures in the premises appointed for these routines. The protest industry had not been developed to its present stage among the angry young. We did not organise 'sit-ins' as a form of 'demo' against the authorities. We had never heard of a teach-in. Adding ins and outs to verbs was not then a general practice. Those who were competing in games or for prizes were not said to lose out or win out, as is now the fashion. We just lost or won, as we were taught and not taught-in.

Lecture, which should mean a reading, has become a repellent word often used to describe scolding instead of instruction. In a piece of light verse called 'The Surplice Question' Thomas Hood wrote of

> A wife who preaches in her gown
> and lectures in her night-dress.

The gown is not a help to the academic lecture (for which Roget suggested the now extinct prolation), and that should not be true to the name of the word; it is more than a reading from a text. It should have, but rarely does have, some spontaneity and an injection of personality. It has been long and foolishly assumed in scholastic circles that one who has had a first-class career as an undergraduate and has won the post of a lectureship on the way to a professor's chair can be relied on to lecture efficiently with no training in the use of his voice and the technique of communication. So my university experience, which is probably a common one, was of mumbled delivery in a monotone without any awareness that an audience has to be held by some tricks of a trade which must be learned, such as variations of voice, timing and stress in a lively approach.

Even a bad joke may be better than none. It may

save a lecture from becoming a prolation, soporific for those of a dormitive nature or exasperating to those who, staying perhaps reluctantly awake, are exasperated by academic incompetence. The learned person on the dais should realise that he is taking the stage and that, if he can 'put up an act', he can rescue the word lecture from the usual assumption that the audience must put up with no more than is expected from attendance at an educational drill. Walt Whitman wrote, 'I do not give lectures, I give myself.' There is much in that if the self is an acceptable present. The word electuary means a dose of medicine wrapped in a honey or syrup. Given with a coating of humanity and humour the lecture need not be a pill in the curriculum.

Call it a prolation, call it a discourse, call it rather a teach-in if that will help to provide escape from the fidgets and the yawns induced by the formal address delivered as a salary-earning duty.

A valuable alternative to the course of lectures is the group-meeting of teacher and taught in what is now called a seminar. Oxford describes this as a form of instruction 'used in German universities and hence in certain British and American universities, a select group of advanced students assembled for study and research under a professor'. That can indeed be a teach-in. But there cannot be enough of those enlivening seminars when the numbers taking a subject are large. Mass distribution of learning by lectures goes on and becomes increasingly common. Without a touch of brilliance on the dais it can easily be a sleep-in. Enough, I am becoming a lecturer.

Lirripoop

Our short word poop for a fool may be an abbreviation of the trisyllabic nincompoop and lirripoop. The latter was used in the eighteenth century. The person so called was not one of the complete blockheads for whom there had been plenty of picturesque names such as numskull, clodpoll, and jobbernowl. The lirripoop had learning and lacked common-sense. The erudition of this wise fool, now levelled to be a clot or chump as well as a poop, seems to have been the cause of this engaging dismissal of the academic dolt.

The hood and the long tail of a university gown were both called lirripoops. A shortened form of this, lurry, was also known in the seats of learning. It meant 'something learned by a rote or a lesson'. Milton wrote of the 'liturgies and lurries of a priest'. There was a slide downwards when the lirripoop was demoted to be the cord of a gown and then any piece of string, including a shoe-lace. So the word could be applied to the wiseacre on his way to give or receive instruction and to his 'correct academic attire' from head to foot.

Loo

The lingo of the lavatory has been levelled. I do not now expect to hear any anxious enquiry for the whereabouts of the privy or the 'retiring room'. The common loo prevails. In a revue not long ago a newly made baroness announced in song 'I am looking for "the ladies" in the Lords'. She might now mention her need for the loo. Even a duchess,

77

who once might have asked for the cloak-room, would now be looking unashamedly for the loo. No doubt the sanitary provision in the Upper House for both sexes qualifies for the description 'de luxe'.

That came to mind because a friend once told me that his housekeeper had come happily home one evening with the announcement that she had had a grand time in a 'cinema de loo'. She was not alluding to the majestic plumbing and pottery in her palace of pleasure. General luxury was what she had in mind. There are now many claims to de luxe surroundings (or de loo, if that pronunciation is preferred). The luxury label is favoured by estate agents. At what point and with what amenities a flat becomes a luxury flat varies. The necessary standard of splendour appears to be modest, an adjective not applicable to the rent demanded.

The loo has largely replaced the lavatory and the lav in current conversation. At one time schoolchildren were expected to use the genteel word toilet. I once walked among the woodlands and boskage of a remote part of Hampstead Heath with a boy who was too polite to 'answer natural call', as the Victorians used to put it, amid the bushes. He enquired, 'Is there a toilet here?' That was some time ago. Now I think he would use a shorter word.

In Britain the Ladies and the Gents have levelled the social distinctions observed elsewhere in the naming of what Americans sometimes discreetly call a 'comfort station'. In Germany there used to be indications of differing quality by labelling some loos *Herren* or *Damen* and others *Männer* or *Frauen*, with the dreadful word Abort kept for the lowest grade.

I recollect an interesting mixture of crude provision of a loo with a polysyllabic title. This I met when wandering among the plebeians on Epsom Downs on Derby Day. By paying my penny I could step behind a rough piece of canvas whose proprietor shouted the word 'accommodation'. That name brings one back to the old-world commode, often an elegant piece of furniture, as handsome as useful when loos were scarce.

The vocabulary of evacuation in Tudor times had been crude. There were jakes and stools. Then Sir John Harington's introduction of the water-closet to Queen Elizabeth's palace of Whitehall was regarded as a novelty which in fact it was not. Archaeological research has established that the loos of the Minoans in Crete were flushable as early as 1500 B.C. The W.C. was no innovation when at last it reached London in a few august homes. Sanitary progress was slow. In Dickensian times there were far more earth closets than watered ones and their contents were piled up in the Mounds whose contents were saleable, as Mr Boffin in *Our Mutual Friend* well knew. There were still very few loos 'de luxe' in the Victorian heyday as J. B. Priestley has called the eighteen-fifties.

Maverick

The maverick is now quite often appearing in accounts of queer conduct and political deviation. He began in fact as an animal accidentally at large and not a man or woman who is asserting independence. The name, a Victorian importation from the Wild West, came from a Mr Samuel A. Maverick of Texas who carelessly omitted to brand his calves. They wandered in anonymous freedom and so the word was attached to 'loners' of all kinds. When Mr Richard Taverne, the Independent Labour candidate for Lincoln, won a smashing victory over the official Labour choice in March 1973 he was reasonably spoken of as a maverick. The adoption of that name in England, where few have ever heard of its founding father, the negligent Samuel, has come at a time when 'Westerns' remain curiously popular among film and television features, and also at a time when defiance of the party caucus and the political machines was widely liked by voters at by-elections.

While Mr Taverne was giving the leaders of his party a sensational jolt, the Tory maverick, Mr Enoch Powell, has not suffered loss of public respect by his readiness to be aloft and aloof. Mavericks are on the wayward march and the title given to them has brought a picturesque word into the language. It is true to its source. They will not become what the tradesmen call 'branded articles'.

Mayhem

'May-day, May-day, brightly breaking.' The merry month should enter so. How chilly that dawn can be has often been discovered by early attenders at the seasonal and choral ritual on the topmost tower of Oxford's Magdalen College. On meeting mayhem, as I frequently do in the reports of violent crime which become more frequent and more horrible as our civilisation marches (or lurches) on, I turn to the dictionary for reassurance that the names preceded by that of the month, once jocund to the poets, will be cordial and comforting. Some of them certainly are not.

The maybug is a cockchafer. May-butter is an unsalted spread 'prescribed for medicinal use'. The may-duke is a sour cherry. Mayweed is another term for Stinking Camomile. Mayhem has nothing to do with the calendar. It is a noun derived from the verb 'maim', 'the crime of crippling a person so as to make him less capable of defending himself or annoying his adversary'. (The verb annoy, which originally implied infliction of serious damage instead of a petty nuisance, is here properly used.) Mayhem once incurred violent retribution in kind. 'By the ancient law of England he that maimed any man whereby he lost any part of his body was sentenced to lose the like part.' So mayhem was a risky enterprise for the mutilators. What they sliced off in hot blood they could lose in cold, having had time to think the matter over. Now the old term has been revived in the newspapers to give a romantic look to any tale of assault and seems to include all degrees of violence, or even rough play. There is something to be said for the revival of this medieval oddity whose arrival in the language Oxford puts at 1492. Whether or not accurately applied it gives the language a lift.

Megalopolitan and Arcadian

Megalopolitan is now applied to Greater London by those favouring a classical and polysyllabic vocabulary. Town-planning, with its conurbations and environmental amenities (or lack of them), has piled up its words as the architects have piled up the office blocks. A recent addition to the talk of the towns and their fringes has been subtopian. When I heard it in discussions I thought it was used by lofty metropolitan persons somewhat contemptuous of suburban development. Naturally one does not expect anything 'super' when a word begins with 'sub'. To my surprise I learned from the *Penguin Dictionary* that a subtopia is 'a suburban area regarded as an ideal place to live in'. This suggests that the 'overspill', quite a simple term for a form of population explosion, can be decanted into a region of unquestionable peace and beauty in contrast with the usual shabby sprawl of megalopolitan expansion. Ideal? Is a new Arcady being created for London's commuters?

The supposedly serene valleys among the mountains in the Peloponnese of Greece, which were known as Arcadia, remind me of a very strange fact. There in the province of tranquillity whose music was the piping of the rustic god Pan a town was built in the year 371 B.C. It was created by uniting a number of primitive villages. Conurbations were still a long way off. But it was proudly called Megalopolis. This happened in the district destined to create the adjective Arcadian which came to mean 'ideally rural' and 'happy in its pastoral innocence'. Ancient Greece was made of small city states, the best of which were isolated enclaves of civilised living. Yet from it has come the epithet for urban monstrosity. William Cobbett, the recorder of his *Rural Rides* in the Home Counties before they became all homes and no country, levelled the pride of Londoners and the language of the planners, when he called the megalopolitan metropolis the 'Wen'.

Arcadian, with a small initial letter, is in its meaning as far from bucolic as it can be. It describes the part of a town furnished with those select, roofed-in, well-windowed and convenient shopping-conduits where the specialists in the costlier antiques, first editions and expensive haberdashery are accustomed to congregate. Piccadilly's Burlington Arcade was a famous centre of arcadian elegance. At one time it was renowned for its seductive ladies on the amorous prowl. If there was a local deity it was Aphrodite not Pan, the god of the Arcadian flocks grazing round the first Megalopolis.

Mugging

In 1972 the newspapers often carried the word mugging in the caption of a news-story. There had been a series of robberies with violence, sometimes including murder, committed by young ruffians who carried knives and were ready to stab as well as cosh their nocturnal victims. The word for this villainy was new to me and surprising since a mug or muggins had long been a slang name for a simpleton with no suggestion of savagery. He was an ass, not an assassin. But the mugging of the new muggers was not slang for long. It was a term used by judges passing justifiably severe sentences in the Courts of Justice.

I learned that I was wrong in thinking this a new arrival. Eric Partridge tells us that the verb to mug has a criminal past. From 1800 onwards it was slang for 'to swindle, to rob especially by the garrotte'. That was a mid-Victorian term meaning to throttle in order to rob. The knife or dagger has replaced the strangulating cord. Garrotte has a suggestion of frenchified scholarship. The new mugging has no such distinction; it is a word as ugly as the deed.

Nut

We gently and rightly refrain from calling madmen mad. The vocabulary of insanity has become tactfully evasive. The madhouse, once a Bedlam or a lunatic asylum (callously spoken of in slang as a loony bin), has the hopefully therapeutic title of a mental hospital. But the levellers have made use of the monosyllables. They now say of one politely called a mental case that he is batty or that he is bats. That is a truncation of a previous description of a wandering mind, 'Bats in the belfry'. Although 'a bee in his bonnet' remains common vernacular I never hear it said of one supposed to be demented, 'He's bees'.

When I am listening to a crime story on the air I frequently hear a detective suggest that the offender is a nut. That of course is short for a nutcase, one who is off his nut or head and is 'crackers', short for crack-brained. It may be added of one so daft and 'round the bend' that his proper place is in a 'nuttery' not a gaol. The brevities abound. For those who are not afraid of a long word there is erudite mention of aberration, alienation and hallucination.

The last is puzzling. It is suggested that the root of it was alucination, turning away from the light. We are back in the darkness of the infested belfry. The victim is bats. To say that he has a screw loose has been a familiar description of the dignified alienation.

Lunatic means moon-struck and there is still some belief that those who fall asleep with a full moon shining on them are liable to be mentally afflicted. It is natural to suppose that darkness is more dangerous to reason than the lucination whose absence was thought to produce the vagrant mind of the hallucinated. Most, however, agree with Ben Jonson's salute to Diana, as a 'goddess excellently bright' who may bless us with her radiance. It occurs to me that none of the American astronauts who trod on Diana's face and scientifically examined her wrinkles complained of any mental disturbance.

Panic

We frequently read that 'the crowd panicked'. With the appalling amount of recent violence and bomb-planting it could have had ample reason for making a hurried flight, so various and frightening were the acts of public mayhem. But the terrified had no right to the verb, which the dictionaries do not admit. This, however, may be one of the cases in which we have to accept an error under pressure of constant usage. Surrenders must be made when the look or sound of a word has completely altered its meaning. That has happened in the case of the Italian furore, which means a burst of enthusiastic approval and is now everywhere used to signify exactly the opposite. If I read in one of the news-papers known as quality that a Minister's statement in the House of Commons produced a furore when he raised a hostile uproar, I do not bother to write to the editor to complain of a solecism. The con-fusion with fury has gone far enough and wide enough to prevail. So too, I fancy, with inchoate, which means in a state of beginning or preparation without any implication of disorder. Its appearance is so close to that of chaos that a bungled policy is now called inchoate without challenge from the devotees of the correct. And so with the verb panic.

The noun panic comes from the ancient Greek Arcadia, which was previously mentioned as the haunt of the god called Pan. At first there was nothing fearsome about him. He was indeed pro-tective, the patron of the shepherds and herdsmen. He was also artistic and invented the syrinx, a flute favoured by the pastoral musicians. That seems harmless enough but his physical blend of man and goat caused him to be regarded as something of a goblin and even an unholy terror who might pounce alarmingly when he was expected to be a benign guardian.

So the crowds still panic, with a 'k' added when the past tense is used. I suppose it was this alliteration which made Barrie choose the Arcadian name for his Kensington stage favourite, the whimsy child who refused to grow up. I have always been allergic to Master Pan since I never saw the play until I had put away childish things. This Peter was neither goatish, nor a musician nor a flautist like the mythical Greek original. If I were invited to see his escapades again, despondency and alarm would set in. I admit that I am almost unique in resisting his appeal. Charismatic, as we now say, to myriads of all ages, he leaves me sourly apprehensive of a further meeting. At the thought of it I am driven to the verb that has forced its way into our language. I panic.

Politician

The word comes out with a contemptuous hissing sound and the name has been in disrepute down the centuries. The adjective mere may be attached to it. That is comparatively gentle. Shakespeare's choice was far less kind. King Lear, in the bitter tragedy of that name, cries out:

> Get thee glass eyes;
> And, like a scurvy politician, seem
> To see the things thou dost not.

86

It can be said that he was distraught with his suf-
ferings when he thus dismissed the whole class as
frauds. But Hamlet was completely sane when he
said of a skull dug up in the burial-ground of
Elsinore, 'This might be the pate of a politician,
one that would circumvent God'. And so it went
on. Dean Swift said that a man who could make
two ears of corn or two blades of grass grow where
one grew before was more deserving of mankind's
admiration than 'the whole race of politicians'.
The statesman might or might not be statesman-
like. His followers whose support kept him in office
were thought of as crafty scoundrels who, as Hamlet thought, were getting round God, that is breaking all the accepted rules of morality.

In the public opinion of today the member of
the British Parliament is still thought of as a second-
rate citizen. Yet, when applicants for a seat in that
assembly are being chosen, there is a rush of those
eager to become politicians. The candidates are
chosen by the local party leaders, who are known
by the strange name of a caucus. This curious word
came to Britain not only from America but from
the oldest inhabitants of that continent, the Red
Indians. One of their tribes, the Algonquins, had a
word in their language, *cau-cau-as*, meaning one
who advises or encourages.

The language of politics has further peculiari-
ties. The selected candidate 'stands' for a seat in
the House of Commons and, if he wins it, he may
have nowhere to sit since there are not enough seats
for all the members and, on a crowded day with an
important debate, he may have to do some more
standing. Order is maintained in the House by a
chairman called the speaker, and he never makes a
speech.

The politician also suffers from the terminology

of party discipline, in which the word Whip is used for an instruction to vote as the party leaders decide. This seems to regard the member as an unruly cur or member of a pack of hounds.

To be a politician in Britain is to carry a name which, if it does not actually stink, carries a nasty smell. It is usually very unfair. He who chooses this career has to be a day and night worker during the sessions of Parliament. He has to keep in touch with his constituents, listen to and if possible remedy their grievances. If he succeeds as a speaker he may rise to hold office and become a Very Important Person, but then he is a target for the critics in the press and speakers on radio and television.

He cannot rely on respect. A *Diary of the Years 1965–67* appeared in 1972. It was written by Mr Cecil King, who was once the head of a powerful group of popular papers and a Governor of the Bank of England. He had managed to have frequent talks with all the party leaders and note what they said. His opinions of them were damning, destructive and set down without mercy. Harold Wilson was violently attacked. Other Labour Ministers were 'failures and total duds'. One was 'so dim as to be hardly noticeable'. On the Conservative side 'Mr Heath has no understanding of politics'. The tirade continued. On neither side, we were told, is there anyone fit to govern the country. All this abuse was thrown at men who can be ranked as statesmen. What would Mr King have said about their followers, the mere politicians?

Must the language of politics be such bad language? Political democracy, of which Britain is proud and which it is determined not to lose, demands drudgery in committees in the parliamentary routines. Its workers deserve some gratitude and fewer growls.

Poetese and Damsel

Poetese is not a dictionary word but has become a familiar dismissive term for diction once thought proper to poetry and kept long in use by the poets when it had become out of date in normal speech and writing. There never was a time when old curios and furniture were more expensive and yet more eagerly purchased in the shops selling antiques. There has been an excellent and I hope popular television feature with questioning of experts and amateurs about the origins, dates and present valuation of rare and precious articles lent for the occasion by private owners and museums. But a verbal antique is so far from being treasured that it is despised.

Some of the relics of poetese have sensibly been dropped. The use of thee and thou became absurd when nobody was speaking in that way to his or her dear one. Lingering forms of old verbs, as in doest or dost, have also been dropped by the versifiers. But some preference for extinct words remained at the beginning of this century. On rereading Rupert Brooke, for example, I find that he used an extinct Elizabethan adjective immote for unmoved or unmovable. He surely would not have used that term when writing in prose.

I was set thinking about that when I came across damsel in the poetry of the past. It had a long run from Edmund Spenser's 'Epithalamion' with its

Come now, ye damozels of delight,

by way of Coleridge's vision of 'a damsel with a dulcimer' in his 'Kubla Khan' and so on to Rossetti's Blessed Damozel (with the zed restored) in which poetese abounds. His angels 'sing to their citherns and citoles'.

To speak of a damsel is now a jest. But it is a word which might have survived, being far preferable to the ugly single syllable of girl which is more a grunt than a word, a surly name for its possibly charming owner. I suppose damsel and maiden are beyond rescue now, but when the bards of today, who would not like to be so described, got rid of the verbal antiques they banished some pleasant-sounding relics from the slopes of Parnassus, a mountain probably odious to them because of its association with the Muses who gave their name to our museums. For them the rejected poetese had become a musty nuisance. But there are things worth saving among its period curios.

Poodle

The poodle dog arrived in the English homes and in miniature form took its place on English laps at the beginning of the nineteenth century. There was a verb, to poodle, meaning to splash about in pools and puddles. The sound of the name suggests a sticky mess whereas paddle, usually applied to a dip of feet in the sea on a sandy shore, has a cleaner suggestion. It would have been kinder to the aquatic animal, which is fond of mingling immersion with exercise, to call him a paddle, but the cooing sound of the two oos suggests an affectionate relation between man and beast. This, my experience for ten or more years, has been delightfully maintained.

The poodle is a natural and very agile performer and exhibitionist. It is no effort for him to stand on his hind legs and he can be taught to turn somersaults. I hate the spectacle of performing animals in circuses and music-halls but it is likely that poodles are those most likely to caper at command without cruel pressure. In one of Georges Simenon's best novels there is a much-loved poodle who has been taught to turn somersaults backward and loves to display his ability in that antic.

An early mention of the poodle's versatility occurs in the light verse of the short-lived Winthrop Mackworth Praed (1802–1839). He wrote an amusing piece, 'Farewell to the Season', in which he remembers in August the follies of fashionable London in June and July. Of his coming vacation he says:

> While my mistress is bathing at Brighton
> I'll angle immensely for trout.

('Immensely' is fascinating. Did he expect a basket loaded with two-pounders?) Among the modish absurdities of Mayfair he includes some curious specimens diverting the gentry in their clubs and the ladies in their salons. There is

> A macaw at Boodles
> Which is held to have something to say

and

> Miss Splenetic's musical poodles
> Which bark, Batti, Batti, all day.

Poodles, I know, can yap. Their voices are not the best of their many engaging possessions. Musical I have not found them. Had Miss Splenetic in

91

addition to her petulance a taste for canine tuition in harmonics and a frustrated resolve to improve on Batti, Batti?

Porn

When I was young and eager to read the books, completely innocent by today's standards, which a schoolboy had then to keep hidden, we called it simply, shortly and accurately smut. Since then the name has been elevated to Pornography. Now, since the sub-editors of popular papers need short words to fit into the narrow space of their news-story captions, three syllables have been lopped off and Fleet Street has given us Porn. In 1971 the Earl of Longford, once the Roman Catholic leader of the Labour Party in the House of Lords, en-listed a team of conscientious colleagues of all parties to investigate and report on the activities of the smut-pedlars. They also considered the state of the law in the matter of obscene publications. This well-intentioned exercise was deemed to be laughable by the progressive permissives and the earl was dismissed as laying a wind egg and derided as Lord Porn.

Before its entry on pornography, Oxford includes in its dictionary pornocracy. This is defined as 'the dominating influence of the harlots, specially the gov-ernment of Rome during the first half of the tenth century'. This strange information about the history of the Eternal city and the papacy gives the feminine influence a curiously late start. If Aspasia got her word in when Pericles was planning the power and glory of Athens in the fifth century B.C. pornocracy was achieving something of historic value. But putting dates to the dominion of the élite courtesans and their less exalted sisters is non-sensical. They have long been called the members of the world's oldest profession. Stanley Baldwin well described the habits of the pornocrats. They seek and obtain power while rejecting and escaping from responsibility. It is an easy and rewarding way of life.

Pornography is defined as the 'Description of the life, manners, etc., of prostitutes and their patrons; hence the suggestion or expression of obscene or unchaste subjects in literature or art'. How far does that take us? Not far, since the old-fashioned smut runs into new-fashioned smog which recently became a dictionary word for the filthy mixture of smoke and fog. On the matter of obscenity the lawyers are stumbling about in a fuliginous mess of words which defy clear and easy interpretation. It has been established in the courts that obscenity is an offence if it shows 'a tendency to deprave and corrupt'. That only leads to arguments about the nature of depravity and corruption and to the counter-plea of the permissive advocates that if a piece of writing has literary quality it cannot deprave. But who is to be the arbiter of literary excellence? The smut-smog keeps growing thicker. The Longford Report adds that a 'book, magazine or play should be taken to be obscene if its effect taken as a whole is to outrage contemporary standards of decency or humanity accepted by the public at large'. Once more the air is no clearer. What are the standards of 'the public at large'? To judge by the words used in places of public assembly, which include football matches as well as the 'demos' of free-spoken or free-screaming protest groups, anything goes in the estimation of the common man and his girl-friends. Doubtless the champions of Women's Lib demand equality in the right to use what language they like and to read pornography without stint.

This is not a book about social and legal reform. The subject is the English vocabulary. So back to words. Pornocracy and pornography come to us from ancient Greece where a *porne* (pronounced porn-ee) meant the kind of woman whom we charitably call loose. The number of names applied to them in our language has been large and sometimes picturesque or grotesque. (I think of Shakespeare's kicky-wicky, but on looking that up I am told that it may be 'a jocular term for a wife'.) At the social summit of the sinful class is courtesan. That word was at first a synonym for a courtier and later was applicable to both sexes. The women won and the word was specially attached to the wantons who enjoyed dominance without duties. It was observed in 1607 that 'your Whore is for every rascal, but your Curtizan is for your Courtier'. So the names multiply, sometimes with a flourish of Latinity, as in Ben Jonson's fricatrice. Down and down we come from the Tudor doxies to the trollops, tarts, and the dolls doted on by guys. The population of the porn country is too vast for detailed scrutiny, but one of the historic denizens has been the harlot. With her, whose etymological origin is one of the numerous 'obscures', we also meet him. The definition begins 'lad, young fellow, base fellow, knave, vagabond'. Not till the sixteenth century did women join 'the baddies'. Shakespeare, in making Falstaff speak of 'the harlotry players', was being faithful to the old meaning since his colleagues on the stage of his time were all men. But for the most part in his plays the noun is feminine. For those who speak in damning denunciation it makes a fine dismissive sound, as also does a resounding taunt of whore. The lingo of the porn has infinite curiosities for those who find

94

the terminology of vice to be a more attractive study than the cool vocabulary of virtue. Why, incidentally, the Elizabethan strumpet? Yet again, 'origin obscure'.

Preserves

The levellers can be thanked for getting rid of some refined and pretentious names once thought to look well on a menu. In hotels and railway restaurant cars the list of breakfast dishes often ends with preserves. That can be defended as an inclusive word which covers marmalade as well as jam. But it was also employed owing to the snobbery once prevalent in the kitchens and larders of the genteel. In their homes one was invited to luncheon, not asked to lunch. Beside the cutlery was a serviette instead of a napkin. Fruit was served with finger-bowls.

We are always in a jam nowadays whether in traffic, on a crowded pavement, or in a tangle of domestic chores. The edible jam has the same origin. It was fruit mushed and crushed in order to produce the preserve. The word, short, simple and common, looks just right for the juvenile joy which it provides when spread on the cereal, slice or slab at the family table. It is certainly not deterrent if one can expect strawberries as the ingredients with plums and gooseberries kept well away from the boiling. It is a good, coarse cousin to pudding and pie which the addicts of preserves prefer to call sweets. It is odd that pastry with jam on it or fruit under it could be called a tart since that, as an adjective, has long meant bitter. Presumably wanton girls were and still are called tarts for the pleasure they provide and not with any thought of sharp and bitter conversation.

There is another and a remaining example of gentility among the sweeteners. That is the substitution of golden syrup for the old and excellent word treacle, a name originally given to a therapeutic balm, used especially for the relief of snakebites. As such it had a place in theology before it was established in the grocer's shop. A prolific author, the monk John Lydgate of Bury St Edmunds, wrote early in the fifteenth century that the name of Jesus was 'holsomest tryacle'. Much later it became in the dictionary 'the uncrystallised syrup produced in the refining of sugar', and on the table a glorious sticky alternative to jam. Syrup has been handicapped by childish memories of after-party purging with California Syrup of Figs.

Another in the rightly disliked preserve class is condiment. It has its utility as a group-word covering 'anything of pronounced flavour used as a relish'. But few would now say in the home, if mustard, pepper and salt had not been put on the table, 'Where are the condiments?', or, seeing no jam or marmalade at breakfast-time, 'Where are the preserves?'

Promenade

One of the most enduring of the English Music Hall songs is that of the seaside lover,

> I do like to walk along the Prom, prom, prom,
> Where the brass-band plays Tiddly-om, pom,
> pom.

I am old enough to have heard it put breezily

across by the first of its singers, Mark Sheridan, whose name linked him with Georgian Bath and streets of dignity. Stately among such roads is esplanade, which began as a Spanish fortification and became peacefully the strolling ground between the sands, the Grand Hotels and less costly Private Hotels—no boarding houses now—of the popular 'maritime resorts'. There have been several names for this kind of unwalled thoroughfare. 'A walk along the Front' suggests to me unimpressive lodging houses and a chilly breeze. Better is marine parade on whose benches there is an implicit invitation to stop and sun oneself or apricate, if I may revive the use of a nice old verb for turning oneself into a human apricot.

Promenade is almost as impressive as esplanade. The former was originally a carriageway since the Latin verb *prominare* meant to drive a beast forward. At Blackpool in an open horse-drawn vehicle the apricants who are too old or too lazy for parading on foot can still be promenaders in the original sense of carriage-folk. The walkers took the word over and at the Albert Hall's Promenade Concerts the enraptured mass of listeners includes the many who cannot perambulate and must be 'standing' devotees. Having been schooled in Cheltenham I remember its broad, fountained and tree-lined main street, the Promenade, with appreciation. I am also grateful to that academic town for its amusing pedantry in naming another street with geometrical accuracy Parabola Road. (A parabola is curvaceous, being 'one of the conic sections'.) The lexicographers have much more to say about that, but the detailed definition is too dry to suit the seemly architecture of a town through which the late Georgians and early Victorians were promenaded in their coaches, chariots and cabriolets. It seemed a pity that in my time

97

the local name for the still horse-drawn descendant of these chariots was the miserable 'fly'. Both Promenade and Parabola deserved vehicles with consequential and not contemptuous titles. Cheltenham's Promenade was levelled to be 'the Prom', but Parabola Road did not become 'the Prab'.

The street-names of Britain are a strangely mixed company. Of the European importations we have retained plenty of Avenues. The Piazza, once the glory of seventeenth-century Convent (now Covent) Garden, has gone. The medieval link of Whitehall with the City of London, once 'La Straunde', has become the Strand. The humblest of names are still attached to streets of solid dignity or sumptuous prosperity. Nobody has suggested that Park Lane should be Park Avenue. Heriot Row is the modest label of one of Edinburgh's spacious and gardened streets. Pastoral history lingers on in the midst of cities. The lawyers sit at their desks in Lincoln's Inn Fields, not Lincoln's Inn Square. Nothing could be more urban than Shepherd's Market. There are Gardens where no horticulture is to be seen. Diamonds, not daffodils, abound in Hatton Garden.

We must be loyal to those old aliens, the Spanish esplanade and the French promenade. The first adds pleasure to the intake of ozone, the second to a stroll among the shops.

Propinquity

Neighbour is an odd-looking word and has a friendly sound, but the proverbs and adages have been unkind to it. We have been told that good fences make good neighbours and that the best neighbours are distant ones. Strictly the neighbour should not be an immigrant or an arrival from a distant part of the country. His name indicates that he was born near to us.

Despite the cynics there is much stress on neighbourly relations when new housing is being planned. Environs are neighbouring places and environment is a word now always in the papers. The vocabulary of adjacency and vicinity is solid and solemn. I prefer propinquity to proximity. The former noun has a lonely place in the dictionary. It has no companion adjective or verb. Advertisements of desirable houses do not call them propinquitous to a railway station and a bus route. Nor do we grumble that among our neighbours we have some very odd propinks. But propink would sometimes be a good description of our environmental personnel, sharers in our vicinage as a Government Department might choose to call them.

Provincial

Mr John Counsell, who has preserved and enhanced the good name of the Theatre Royal at Windsor, has explained in his programme magazine that the adjective provincial should not be applied to playhouses outside London. He politely calls it patronising. It is in fact a slur. Regional should be, and is, rightly taking its place. There are now more and better planned playhouses being built away from the capital and its supposedly prestigious West End. If provincial implies a sneer they deserve to be spared so inept an epithet.

The first provinces were the parts of the Roman Empire which lay outside Italy. So the provincials were outsiders from the start. They have ever since been the victims of metropolitan snobbishness and the arrogance of those living in capital cities. The idea of second-rate quality was oddly exemplified out of town in the Horseback Halls of the English countryside where those chasing the fox with any but the fashionable packs in 'the shires' were loftily dismissed as 'huntin' in the provinces'. Scholars joined the sportsmen in their contempt of the supposedly ignorant and boorish provincial. To Dr Johnson the word meant 'rude, unpolished'.

The 'provincial press' has been a derogatory name for newspapers published in the great cities away from London, in the big industrial centres and in the capitals and major towns of Scotland, Ireland, and Wales. Their standard of journalism was and often remains higher than some of the products of Fleet Street. C. P. Scott of the *Manchester Guardian* disliked and, I think, barred in his columns mention of 'the provinces' and the use of the adjective provincial. The magnetism of London drew off first-rate newspaper men who made their names known beyond as well as in their own cities. Their move was not always rewarding. London cost more while it paid more. Its supposed prestige was not certain to be a satisfying compensation.

A region began regally as a form of realm. If regional has lost some status it has not fallen as far as provincial, which is linked with parochial in the disdain of the 'very superior person'. Henry James in his life of Hawthorne said of Thoreau, 'He was worse than provincial. He was parochial.' Not being in love with the megalopolitan life of today I think of parochial with some fondness for small places and their local pride.

Pudicity

The word meaning modesty or chastity is as rarely
met in print as its implicit virtues are encountered
in the world of entertainment. I do not agree that
the frequent use of the four-letter words in newspapers and novels or in the theatre is one of
'the commendable blows struck for progress'. Nor
am I convinced that the average human body is so
shapely that its exposure is inevitably exciting or
likely to offer a vision of supreme loveliness.

Wearing clothes may be thought by the devotees
of strip-tease to be a miserable surrender to
decorum. But dress can also be at some times a
pleasing form of decoration. That has to be said
with a considerable reservation. In those streets of
central London and even in Mayfair where once
there was pride of appearance there is so much drab
dullness and even sluttishness of attire that the
spectacle can hardly be called enlivening or en-
trancing. But those adjectives are absurd if applied
to a parade of nudes in a sleazy cellar. I speak from
hearsay, not being a sampler of subterranean
pleasures in Soho's 'joints' where pudicity is least
likely to be found.

There is another effective but rarely used word
of Latin origin to describe the direct opposite of
pudicity. That is lubricity, which first meant slip-
periness and then slid downwards and became a
synonym for lewdness and lasciviousness. The pro-
testers against 'porn' need some more adjectives to
add to their hard-worked denunciation of 'cor-
rupting influences'. A lubricious exhibition would
enlarge their vocabulary of indictment. When a
central London theatre once respected for the excellence of its plays by the best authors had a

long-running display of eroticism blatantly entitled *The Dirtiest Show in Town*, lubricity was in the money as well as in the limelight.

When there was still some pudicity surviving, the sexual organs, which were not then on public view, were known as pudenda, a formidable term. I remember a College conversation on the respectable subject of curious figures in English history in which a hitherto silent member intervened in verse. Having briefly murmured

> Henry the Eighth, the Faith's Defender,
> Had astonishing pudenda,

he said no more, being usually a taciturn man, sometimes sardonic but as far from prolixity as his reticence could carry him. He had contributed concisely and in language which did not offend against the pudicity proper in academic surroundings to the physiological interpretation of history.

I gather from the publicity of the film-trade that in certain cinemas, as now on certain stages, the pudenda are not kept invisible. Fig leaves have drifted away on the winds of change. Those liable to be afflicted with smut-shock must reconcile themselves to an emended version of Horatio's lines to the dying Hamlet

> Absent thee from pudicity awhile
> And in this brash world draw thy breath in
>   pain.

Brash, incidentally, has a variety of meanings: as a noun it is 'an acidulous belching from the stomach'. As an adjective it means brittle, bumptious, rough and insolent. With the last of these it is a crude cousin of lubricious.

Rhomboideus

That adjective was used by a friend when I asked him about the new 'architectural development' which was to replace an old and admittedly wilting example of London's Georgian classical style. Brief research informed me that he was using an adjective known to Oxford and that a rhomb is 'a plane figure having four equal sides and the opposite angles equal, two being acute and two obtuse; also a single, lozenge-shaped object or formation'. A rhombohedron is 'a solid figure bounded by six equal rhombs'.

Into the structure expected to dominate the old street some hundreds of 'the clerical establishment' will soon be pouring. Previously a few dozen were every day accommodated there. The rush-hour scamper for inadequate transport, bad then, will be far worse. There are consolations. Those rhomboideusly accommodated will have lifts. (We are not yet so much influenced by the American addiction to the classics that we must 'operate the elevator' instead of working the lift.) They will have an enormous number of windows in their glass cage.

Windows? Nothing so common. Extensive fenestration is now the correct description. Or, to vary the lingo, the denizens of the new rhombic city will be the beneficiaries of ample vitrification. The English of the master-builders runs as high as their cement. Fifty years ago there was a cult of the solid mass in the studios of the advanced artists who were known as Cubists. A landscape, they maintained, if properly seen by the discerning eye, is a cluster of solid lumps. The rhomb was not then in vogue among those who were determined to find nothing gently curvaceous in Nature's hills, woods and forests. Cubes for them! Now the urban view is being similarly rectified. Rhomboideus? The levellers have their own name for this style of the developers. Egg-box, they say. In this I am on their side.

Saga

Like the cod-fish it comes from Iceland. It was 'a composition in prose written during the Middle Ages'. Norway shared in this authorship. Some of Ibsen's first and now forgotten plays were saga stuff. The word came to mean a series of stories without any necessary Scandinavian connection. Kipling wrote of a talkative man who 'delivered himself of the saga of his own doings'. When John Galsworthy's astute publisher collected his novels about the Forsyte family and issued them in one volume as *The Forsyte Saga* they had an enormous sale in many countries, thanks to his skilful promotion. No doubt the word saga helped. Though an import it suggested, with justice, a vast stretch of English life.

Journalism has adopted saga with some odd results. I have just read in my local paper about a new school in which some gas-leaks were found. For five days the pupils had to stay at home while the officials of the Gas Board nosed around, probed the pipes, went away, came back, went away again and at last put things right. The description of these tardy operations of no great public interest started with 'The saga began'. Our suburb might have been in the world of the Vikings. The reporter was not letting his tale of incompetent dilly-dally seem trivial. I saluted his resolve to make 'a good story' by beginning with an old, heroic, and romantic word.

Smug

During a club conversation about politicians I heard it said by one who should know, since he meets many of them in his position as a librarian at Westminster, that 'all MPs are smug'. I took it that he meant complacent and self-satisfied. It is an ugly little adjective of whose source the lexicographers admit their ignorance. Here again is the curt confession, 'origin obscure'. What is certain is that its meaning has been greatly changed. If we had been talking about a Victorian Parliament the mention of smugness would have been complimentary not derisive since a tidy and well-dressed man was known as smug during the last century. So Thackeray used it of an officer who could finely wear a fine uniform. The application to a person unduly pleased with himself has now completely ousted the idea of the man with a Savile Row suit.

There was a coincidence in our chat since one of the MPs mentioned has a double reputation. He is said to have a high opinion of his own talents and importance. He is also a dandy in a place where the sartorial standards are now low. He may fairly be called smug with both past and present meanings of the word. It is unlikely that he was ever the smug of schoolboy slang who shunned playground and tuck-shop company to concentrate on his books and to be despised as 'a swot'.

Solicitress and Esses

When this name for a feminine lawyer appeared in *The Times* it was attacked by some correspondents and defended by others. In one letter to the editor the word was described as 'hideous' and solicitrix was suggested as an alternative. Is that more agreeable to eye and ear? It may be urged on its behalf that it would at least diminish the chance of a highly educated lady engaged in a legal career being confused with a prostitute. Solicitors are members of a respected profession, and are with very few exceptions well conducted, but the verb solicit has been applied in the law-courts to street-walkers importuning potential customers with invitations to lechery. Accordingly solicitress might be a name easily misunderstood and disastrous to a respectable practitioner (or conductress?) of legal business.

The word would have been accepted and even welcomed by H. W. Fowler, whose *Dictionary of Modern English Usage* is widely taken to be the supreme and generally approved authority on that subject. The champions of Sex Equality were at one time levellers and curtailers of language. They wanted to share with men their designations of occupation. They would not be authoresses or poetesses. They wished to be poets and authors. 'They regarded', said Fowler, 'the distinction as derogatory to them and implying inequality between the sexes. An author is an author. That is all that concerns the reader and it is impertinent curiosity to want to know whether the author is male or female.' Thus Fowler stated their case before he opposed it.

He was no leveller. He liked long polysyllabic

creations. He maintained that 'any word that does the work of two or more by packing several notions into one is a gain'. The more civilised a language, the more such words it possesses. He further argued that since women were constantly entering new spheres of work, feminine forms of what he called 'vocation-words' were more and more needed. He thought it 'amazing that a woman-doctor should not be called a doctress'. He then suggested the retention of authoress and poetess and recommended such innovations as teacheress, singeress and danceress. He rejected such aliens as cantatrice and danseuse; he did not mention the operatic diva and the ballerina. I cannot agree with him about singeress and the others of that kind. Plainly he would have welcomed solicitress.

The general usage in the naming of feminine vocations and those engaged in them is confused. In some cases the French form has become familiar. On the stage we have tragediennes and comediennes. Those of the latter class who specialised in gay and charming entertainment, especially in the parts of coquettish maid-servants, were once called 'soubrettes'. The 'ette' termination has been chiefly found in minor occupations. The playgoer does not expect to be thrilled by a tragediette when an usherette has taken him to his seat. In some cases the female performer has no distinguishing termination. In circuses and music-halls the daring young woman on the flying trapeze is an acrobat and not an acrobatess, as Fowler might have called her.

The campaigners for Votes for Women were suffragists and not suffragettes as they came to be unkindly called. Workers in professions which demand high qualifications have been rightly spared inclusion in the 'ette' class. Doctorettes and teacherettes are unthinkable. Whatever our reaction to solicitress, solicitette would not be endurable.

No move has been made by women called to the Bar to be spoken of as barristresses, much less barristerettes. The prevailing custom is to level most vocation titles and make no sex-distinction. For example women serving as wardens, whether protecting the public against air raids during the war or later watching car-owners beside the meters in the street, have not been wardenesses.

Returning to the law I noted with pleasure the observation made in a letter from the office of the Law Society, which is the professional organisation of the solicitors. Its writer reminded us that 'In the Interpretation Act of 1889 it was laid down that the masculine shall embrace the feminine'. There is decorous gallantry, as well as a legal point, in that. The embrace is chastely technical. No solicitation of a solicitress is suggested. I do not expect to see wardens, though their title is an embracing one, engaged as danceresses in the antics of a 'bunny-hug'.

Fowler's law-giving has been rightly forgotten. Contraltos and sopranos will not become singeresses.

Spatterdash

It arrived on the feet of the gentry, at the end of the seventeenth century. The cover provided by this gaiter was as ample as its name. It was no mere anklet then, but 'a long legging of leather or cloth used to keep the stocking from being spattered with mud while riding'. At that time it was a light-weight alternative to the heavy riding-boot. The definition assumes equestrian wear. But those who walked the streets in wintry and wet weather were also guarding their hosiery with spatter-dashery.

Two hundred years later there was a double process of levelling down. One syllable replaced three and the sizeable gaiter was discarded in favour of the small spat. It was still protective. The muddy unmetalled roads, even with crossing sweepers at work, made a sad mess of a polished boot or shoe. Spats diminished the pollution. Then that usage dwindled. The serviceable became the smart. Spats were dandy's wear. Comedians in foppish parts sported white spats. Bridegrooms and the men attending them at church and wedding parties had to be duly and decoratively spatted below the trousers of the dress suit.

We do not expect to see any of that kind now. A search for them in the haberdashery shops might yield nothing. Yet in 1922 P. G. Wodehouse gave the title *Young Men in Spats* to a collection of short stories in which the members of the Drones Club are the principal characters. Some of them are anonymous and their observations, usually indicating the minimum of mental acumen, are attributed to voices nominated as those of Egg, Bean and Crumpet. These characters of fifty years ago one expects from the title of the book to be constantly spatted. One colour of the spat-wear mentioned in the Club is fawn, but I imagine some flash of white beneath the well-frequented bar.

There has been much change of foot-fashion among the masculine fops. In 1922 to be seen in elastic-sided shoes or boots would have been unthinkable. They had been ridiculed as Jemimas and worn on the stage by pantomime Dames or the players of Old Fogey and fuddy-duddy parts. Then they became known as fashionable Chelseas. Had the Drones Club survived into the nineteen-seventies

the still blessedly productive Wodehouse could
have visualised the modish lounge-lizards as
'Young Men in Jemimas'. Well, if not that, 'Chaps
in Chelseas'.

To the three syllables of the spatterdash the Victorians added two more when they put on their
antigropelos. This magnificent name came from a
long Greek word for damp-defying. The article was
no spat, but a leg-protector. C. S. Calverley introduced it into a parody of the style and vocabulary of
Robert Browning. I doubt whether that young suitor
called on his Elizabeth in Wimpole Street thus
guarded against cold feet. But I can imagine Tennyson so attired and the higher and more consequential clergy of Barchester padding out to a Christmas service with antigropeloid defence against
snow and slush. But I cannot remember any mention by Trollope of this cryptic alternative to the
clearly descriptive spatterdash.

Spectrum

Here is a word which frequently appears in journalism and in the copy written for advertisements.
I have just read an appeal to choose a new outfit
from 'the spectrum of our ready-made suits'. The
parliamentary correspondents at Westminster informed me about changes in the spectrum of the
Conservative, Labour or Liberal policies. In the
former case the spectrum appeared to be a list or
catalogue and in the latter it seemed to mean both
a party programme and its effect upon public
opinion. Investigation was needed.

It was startling therefore to learn from Oxford
that spectrum began its life as 'an apparition or
phantom'. Hamlet, when he asked the angels and

ministers of grace to defend him from what might be a 'goblin damned', could have included spectrum in the extensive vocabulary which he used in his conversations with his father's ghost. After that spooks became less formidably classical and spectres took over from spectrum and spectra. Then came academic promotion. The seventeenth-century scientists were using spectrum to describe 'the coloured band into which a beam of light is de-composed by means of a prism or diffraction grating'. Next came 'the image retained for a time on the retina when turned away after gazing fixedly for some time at a brightly coloured object'. So on to spectrometers and spectroscopes. This was suc-ceeded by the general seizure of the word for any kind of 'image or semblance'. So to write of a poli-tical spectrum became habitual. Then the publicity men adopted it. In their view a reach-me-down suit gains greatly in dignity and probably in price if it is part of an outfitter's spectrum. It is not a word I would choose if asked for a list of my previous books. I would not care to talk of 'the large spec-trum of my publications'. List will do.

It occurred to me that spook might be a popular version of the earliest and spookish spectrum. It has in fact floated in from the Netherlands or old Germany. A youthful friend of mine, a parson's son, with a taste for profanity when away from his home and paternal parish, used to call the Holy Ghost the Sacred Spook. His blasphemy, if that is not too strong a word for his mild jocosity, carried the first kind of spectrum into theology. One thing leads to another when one wonders about words. Blasphemy comes from the Greek word for evil-speaking. Our commonly used blame is a form of it and moved down from sinful impiety to normal censure.

Spree

If we go on the spree we do not know why we call it that. Here is another 'origin obscure'. Ernest Weekley fancied a connection with the Gaelic spraigh which was the name for a cattle-raid used by the Highlanders who thought such forays were fun. That is possible. If so the word had crossed the border and changed its spelling by 1800. In the previous century the revellers spoke of a frisk; 'I'll have a frisk with you', said Dr Johnson.

By a coincidence Berlin's river Spree rises on the borders of Bohemia, which Shakespeare described as a 'desert' and the Victorians regarded as a home of careless gaiety and of artists much given to frisking. Beside the Spree in Prussia's capital the friskers went on the bummel, a word which Jerome K. Jerome introduced to this country when he wrote *Three Men on the Bummel* as a sequel to his immensely successful *Three Men in a Boat*. But bummel did not take root here as spree, whatever its source, did. It suited the writers of music-hall ditties because it made rhyming easy.

> I don't care what becomes of me
> I don't care, for I'm on the spree,
> I'm going to be married in the morning
> So to-night, boys, I don't care.

It was hardly an inspired summons to celebrate, but there was then a popular taste for spree-songs with catchy tunes. At that period the reveller was said to be going on the randan. As in the case of spree, there is no information about the source of that word.

The gossip writers of today tell us of shindigs

and ding-dongs when they give us news of go-ahead gaieties. The former presumably get rough with quarrels to follow the drinking. The latter does not imply more than a fearful clatter of hilarity with no risk of assault amid the animation.

At the beginning of this century those going on the randan were also said to be going on the razzle-dazzle. Later they jived to jazz music. Then came mention of a razz-ma-tazz. When I heard this mentioned on the radio I could not decide whether it referred only to giddy rejoicing. Sometimes there seemed to be the implication of strife amid the capers. The high-spirited will always want to enlarge the old and simple spree.

Squad

Squadron, coming from Italy and first meaning a square formation, has an imposing look and sound. It has been adopted in Britain by Navy, Army and Air Force for units which are not organised in squares. Its use has been specially attached to the cavalry, but Sir Walter Scott wrote of 'mustering clans and squadrons tramping' and so included the infantry. To be called a squadron-leader is to be gloriously titled. But there is a sad descent when squadron is shortened to squad, a horrid little word which has gloomy associations for anyone who has ever been drilled.

Yet it has recently been favoured by journalists writing about sport. I frequently read of footballers who, when up for sale, have changed their teams at a valuation in this curious market of hundreds of thousands of pounds. When one such possessor of 'gold in his boots' moves onward and upward he is now always said to have joined the Chelsea,

Arsenal or Everton squad. That would be suitable if they were on military parade, but I can see no reason why the old team, side and eleven have been dismissed from athletics. Even at Olympic level a runner or jumper of supreme achievement is reported to have joined the British squad as though he were a foot-slogger in a barrack yard. One game leads to another and the aces of the cricket field, whose market price is inconsiderable compared with those of the goal-getters, now belong to a Test Match squad at seigneurial Lord's. That is a deplorable innovation. The heroes of my boyhood were not so demeaned. Nobody could have called the slashing, smashing Jessop or the incomparable Indian Prince 'Ranji' members of the Gloucestershire or Sussex squad. Squadron would do for a side led by masters of their game, but curtailed the word is insulting.

The vogue-words in the sporting gossip have had some queer alterations. Why, for example, is a forward player on the football field now called a striker instead of a goal-getter? The name suggests that he is as ready with his fists as with his feet. To judge by recent misconduct that may sometimes be justified but, if he is normally well-behaved, to call him a striker is libellous.

Square

When I was a boy at school I had to wear a hard, ugly head-piece with a tassel called a mortar-board and commonly known as 'a colleger'. In summer it was replaced by an equally hard and equally uncomfortable straw-hat which blew off on windy days. Both became battered. That was a matter for pride. The decrepit condition of your mortar-board showed your seniority. At Oxford, where it was part of correct academic attire, it was known as a square. That presumably explains its more recent use in slang to describe and deride a solemn and old-fashioned person. Squares of this kind did not jazz, jive, or become hysterical when their ears were assaulted with 'beat' music.

Passing from head to foot we find the adjective further signifying gravity of conduct. The old Puritans, heavily shod, tramped heavily to work and passed by with loathing and contempt the theatres, which they denounced as 'Satan's workshops'. Owing to their massive footwear they were known by the lighter-footed and profane as 'square-toes'.

But to Shakespeare a squarer was not a man of God and good works. He was a quarrelsome fellow and a rip. Beatrice in *Much Ado About Nothing* is curious about Benedick's companion. 'Is here no young squarer now that will make a voyage with him to the devil?' But the adjective had also for Shakespeare its usual meaning of honest, as in square deal. His Cleopatra is mentioned as 'a most triumphant lady, if report be square to her'.

There is another contradiction here. To square an opponent means to get round him, possibly with corruption. The word has squared the circle of meaning. The old squarer squared up when a fight was on. Since then the square has been both a high-brow and a low-dealer. The policeman who allowed himself to be squared would now be called bent, an adjective which has replaced crooked in the films and television series about 'cops' and criminals.

Toady

Reading an article by Bernard Levin approving the kindly citizens of Hemel Hempstead who carried toads across the road to save them from the traffic, I learned of his affection for frogs and toads. The latter creature, as he pointed out, has been hardly used by poets. His zoological name is *Bufo vulgaris* (toad is 'Old English of uncertain origin'). To Shakespeare he was ugly and venomous. He was also a major ingredient in the abominable stew of Macbeth's witches. To Milton he was a nasty 'squatter'.

Soon after Shakespeare's day there came an intrepid man known as a toad-eater. He was 'the attendant of a charlatan employed to eat toads, considered to be poisonous, to enable his master to exhibit his skill in expelling the alleged venom'. The profession is mysterious. For some unexplained reason this consumer of *Bufo vulgaris* became associated with cringing conduct. He became 'a fawning flatterer, parasite, and sycophant'. As such he acquired a new form of his name. He was the toady, used as both noun and verb. This has come to suggest that toads are 'servile with interested motives'. For that there can hardly be any evidence. Fawning or not, they have reason to salute with affection their guardians in Hemel Hempstead.

Travesty

There is something large, almost majestic, in 'the travesty of justice' rolled out by public speakers with a taste for a sounding phrase when the orator is voicing a grievance. (The rank and file of the protest brigade are so sadly lacking in the vocabulary of denunciation that they can only repeat their monotonous and monosyllabic yell of 'Out, out, out'.)

I was surprised to discover that travesty should be transvesty. Its origin is theatrical, not political. The idea of mockery came from the disguise of a comedian who was giving the public the 'low-down' on the high-ups by making their appearance and garments ridiculous. Sexual transvestism has been constant on the stage, seriously and of necessity in the case of the Elizabethan boy players and gaily in the subsequent Pantomimes with their feminine Principal Boys and masculine Dames. In the music-halls, with Vesta Tilley once at the top of the male impersonators, with Mr Danny la Rue as the present Queen of the pretending females, transvestism has been expertly conducted and widely enjoyed. The name of the pretence has suffered in that process by being reduced in our Theatre slang to the curt and rather sordid drag. We should continue to deplore a travesty. We must not have a drag of justice in our oratory and leading articles.

Vacs, Assorted

When I was reading about one of the Wodehouse Wooster's social problems the much-vexed Bertie was physically depressed, drooping in thought or, as he himself put it, 'bending the pensive bean'. What word, he wondered, would suit his perplexity? Was he dithering? He preferred to elevate his vocabulary, a procedure unusual with him. He decided that he was vacillating.

The verb originally meant to stagger bodily. 'To swing away from, to be of uncertain equilibrium' is Oxford's first definition before it moves on to the mental fluctuation. Bertie's protective Jeeves, so strangely well-read, was there with an apt and anglicised quotation from the classics, 'Hither and thither dividing the swift mind'. His employer, comforted with a practical suggestion for coping with the immediate crisis, could abandon vacillation. The bean could be lifted from the shoulders bowed in contemplation. The mind was no longer a vacuum.

Other vacs came to mind. *Vacca* is the Latin for a cow. Hence vaccary for a dairy-farm. The Wodehouse Blandings Castle may have had one beside its notable piggery, but I cannot remember the cow-shed's being so called by the proud owner of the porcine Empress. From vaccary on to vaccinium, 'a plant with edible berries, especially the bilberry'. It may sometimes be a favourite element in the vaccine diet, but usually it is found on moorlands more frequented by nibbling sheep than by munching cows. The latter animal has given us the vaccines injected and derived from the pustules in the teats of cows afflicted with cowpox and later so successfully applied to the prevention of the human smallpox.

A further surprise, remote from the pastoral and medical, is the discovery that vac for a university vacation is recognised by Oxford, a victory for the levellers of our language, among whom Wooster, of Magdalen College, Oxford, was very active in curtailment. Did he leave it as Bertie, B.A.? When he was confronted with the questioning of his exam papers there may have been some vacancy and vacillation in the baffled and bewildered bean.

Vandalism

The itch to grab and steal is natural to the acquisitive human animal. To smash for the sake of smashing has no such rational calculation behind it, but it seems to satisfy some instinctive urge. A general attraction in the great pleasure-ground of Copenhagen, a highly civilised city, was and perhaps still is, the stall at which you could pay a surprisingly small sum for the pleasure of smashing as much crude and coarse crockery as your hurling of the provided missiles could achieve. Though not inclined to violence I have practised and enjoyed this holiday vandalism, but that was some time ago before the prices of everything rose and conservation became a widely supported cult.

Now in Britain there has been a deplorable outbreak of senseless bashing and breaking. The public telephone box is a frequent target for the young devotees of the crazy damage and destruction in which these vandals delight. So they are called by many who could not promptly explain with full historical and geographical detail the dates and stamping-grounds of those people.

Dryden told us

That Goths and Vandals, a rude northern race,
Did all the matchless monuments deface.

(Rude was then a ruder adjective than it is now.) It is curious that in our terminology of barbarism the Goths have largely escaped from the denunciation. Round about 400 B.C. these two Germanic hordes shared the savage inroads which penetrated as far west as Spain after the overthrow of most of the Roman Empire. Incidentally the Vandals have left their name, minus the initial letter, in the southern part of Spain called Andalusia, an unlucky region since it was later overrun by the Moors. The Vandals are now commonly remembered in our police-courts. But nobody calls a smashing oaf a young Goth.

The word Gothicism, used in the eighteenth century, meant 'rudeness, barbarism, absence of polish'. There is nothing very dreadful in the last of these. The glories of the medieval architecture which came to be called Gothic caused a general forgetting of the original brutality and devastation. Horace Walpole used the verb Gothicise for indulgence of one's taste for medieval buildings and their decoration. The Gothic viciousness drifted out of mind. The Vandals' similar sins did not. The Huns, from Asia Minor, had preceded the Germanic invaders and left their name for smashers and grabbers. During the 1914–18 war it was commonly applied in Britain to the German army. But that passed. The lawless louts of today are not so labelled. But they are also spoken of as thugs. These were professional cutthroats and assassins available for hire in India.

The variants for the vandals in our description of ruffianism are hooligans and yahoos. Swift invented the latter. The hooligan was a much later arrival on the English streets and in our vocabulary of violence. Oxford tells us that the word was first used in 1898 and that it was the name of 'an Irish family in S.E. London conspicuous for ruffianism'. They were originally houlihans. So the much-revered Kathleen na Houlihan of the Gaelic legends had some regrettable kinsmen.

What now? We hear of yobs but this is usually the term for unruly and brutish lads. Major crime such as mugging is not necessarily indicated.

Vernacular

The Roman *verna* was 'a home-born slave'. The first vernacular language was that of the servants' hall in a town-house by the Tiber or in a country villa, perhaps that of a settler in Britain. The emphasis moved from the menial to his place of work. 'The vernacular' became the home-talk of a locality, a type of person, and lastly of an occupation or profession. One alternative has been taken from France. The patois is the talk of a district. Another was argot, which was chiefly used of the slang lingo of thieves.

There is an exalted argot, high above the criminal level. That is officialese, the language of government departments. It employs a vocabulary and style of its own. Remembering the Tite Barnacles, the closely connected job-holders in and round Westminster satirised by Dickens in *Little Dorrit*, I invented the name of barnacular for the argot of bureaucracy in which puzzling directives are issued and in which forms are composed for us to fill. Lucidity is rarely achieved. There are some long and learned words to describe its quality. It is opacious. It is obfuscatory. I prefer the simple and dismissive baffle-gab which I think came from America.

Weadle

In a description of a boxing match in the *Guardian* I saw, or rather was shown by my constant colleague in the study of words, Oswald Baxter, a verb new to us both. One of the combatants, it was said, found a task beyond him in 'trying to weadle out the German from his defensive hole'. The term portmanteau is given to words in which several others are condensed. The package-deal in this case seems to contain the elements of the gardener's weeding, the suppliant's wheedling and the hedge-rows' weasel who burrows his way into nooks containing a possible meal. Weasel is a properly nasty name for a creature of similar nature to the ferret and the stoat. It is odd that the latter, also known as the ermine, should be a principal treasure of the furrier's trade and a rival to the diamond as 'a girl's best friend'. A precious coat or stole must often have been weadled out of a wealthy pocket by a woman who knew her way about as cunningly as does the weasel in the field.

What was the weasel which went 'pop' in the old London rhyme? I presume it was slang for money. I expected help from Eric Partridge's *Dictionary of Slang*. His information about weasel tells us that it was the nickname of Robert Cecil, Earl of Salisbury (1563–1612). That crafty statesman could weadle position, wealth and power out of the first Queen Elizabeth.

Wheedle is a verb in the plentiful category of 'original obscure'. Its unknown creator did well, with his smooth, sly and sinuous invention.

Afterword

I have heard voguey used in conversation as an alternative to trendy. So I may be excused for saying that some of the vogue-words grow voguier. Since I wrote about polarisation I have been justified by the increasing refusal to mention any simpler kind of parting or separation. Here is a passage from an article in an educational journal of high repute:

> We are in a period of change when the formal polarisation of a class-room, with rows of pupils facing the teacher, is giving way to a more complex and flexible set of furnishings and organisations that reflect a greater variety of educational objectives and social roles.

The opinion expressed is typically modish in its equalitarian policy and typically prolix and pompous in its style. The teacher must not only be on a level with the taught; he must not confront them since confrontation now suggests conflict. He or she must be in among them, a pal among pals. The idea of a dais in a class-room is reactionary and repellent to the advocate of 'all alike'. I was surprised to find any such distinguishing word as class admitted to his plans for the up-to-date school.

With the opinions comes the language deemed appropriate in the loftier circles of educational advancement. Re-grouping of desks and seats must include complexity and flexibility in the furnishings and organisation which will reflect the educational objectives. Once again we meet the striking contrast between the levelling policy and the un-levelled vocabulary with which it is expounded by those to whom the mere idea or mention of a master must be odious. The Scots used to talk of a dominie. Domination is now unthinkable. In the new 'social roles' of the school-room there must be no assertion of authority by polarisation of the pedagogue from the pupil. I take it that the word pedagogue, though rarely met now, is pardonable since it indicates one who leads, not one who drives, the child. But perhaps even leadership is now suspect in the advanced educational creed which will surely be called its ideology.

Another favourite of our time is identify. I expect to be told that the teacher must identify with the taught. The old meaning of that verb was 'to show or prove the identity of a person or thing'. A criminal, polarised in the dock, was identified by witnesses. The psychologists have altered that. For them to identify means 'to model unconsciously one's behaviour on that of someone to whom one is emotionally attached'. Leading actresses used to speak simply about their work when interviewed. Now they discuss their playing of a part in terms of 'the degree of identification'.

This word is now being used to mean agreement. 'On this point I do not identify with Freud' is the way in which a psychoanalyst makes his declaration of independence. It is customary to start a remark of this kind with the adverb 'basically', which is a particular favourite of broadcasters when they are theorising about theories.

In my Foreword I regretted the present lack of appeal to the ear. This seems to be the more absurd since more and more information, instruction, argument and entertainment are being conveyed through the spoken word by sound radio and by those, including eminent authorities, who supply and deliver scripts for television features. Because they must talk on the level they must concentrate on the meaning, which must be easily intelligible to all. But words are potentially emotive music, and there is little of that in the vocabulary of the talkers on the many subjects now lumped together as sociology. There is no belief that 'the message' will be better conveyed if it is accompanied by a pleasant noise.

There was an old word, verbigeration. Oxford defines it as 'repetition of the same word or phrase in a meaningless fashion'. The name is an old one but the practice remains; in some cases it escalates. Verbosity abides, but without reverberation. To be just audible seems to be the highest ambition of the lecturer or public speaker. The latter may be eager to stimulate enthusiasm when he is pleading for a cause but he avoids the kind of language which was once employed to warm the feelings of an audience. The drums and trumpets of rhetoric are muted. There used to be preachers in the various churches and chapels who drew an audience because they had commanding voices and were not ashamed to use them. The sermon was the one part of a religious service which was not a routine repetition. In it there might be something fresh and so attractive to those who were averse to the too familiar ritual. I surmise that the common clerical complaint of empty churches is partly caused by the absence of the eloquence delivered with the star-quality of a justly popular preacher who knew how to select and how to project his chosen words.

I remember with surprise that, though a young heretic, I went as a boy to hear the Rev R. J. Campbell at the City Temple. He was so much the white-headed hero of the Nonconformists that the picture postcards of his handsome face were frequently displayed among those of the stage's charmers. At Oxford, still more anti-clerical, I went to hear sermons in St Mary's when a fine visiting speaker was booked as the star sermoniser. On the secular front I went to political harangues by the magnetic Lloyd George and by some of the Socialist leaders whose 'gab' was considered to be good value. If Hilaire Belloc was holding forth on any subject his robust rhetoric was a delight to appreciative ears as well as to a sympathetic mind. His discourse, with its rolling of the r's, was a river of sound. A gentler flow, but delicately musical, was the lecturing by Gilbert Murray on any classical theme. So grew my love of 'proper words in proper places', spoken as effectively as they were picked. The broadcasters of today are fashionably 'in the swim', but there is none of the old euphonious flood. Nothing to captivate the ear can be expected from the exposition of an ideology. So I would be grateful if those with much to say weadled out of our ample but neglected vocabulary some musical words which would raise the level, now as unimpressive as a level slice of the Low Countries. Language can have its landscape in which verbal mountains and valleys are gloriously mingled.